A Special Gift

Presented to:

....

From:

....

Date:

....

Stories, Sayings, and Scriptures to Encourage and Inspire

BIG
hugs®
for Women

HOWARD BOOKS
A DIVISION OF SIMON & SCHUSTER
New York   London   Toronto   Sydney

Mary Hollingsworth
Philis Boultinghouse

Personalized Scriptures by
LeAnn Weiss

Our purpose at Howard Books is to:

- *Increase faith* in the hearts of growing Christians
- *Inspire holiness* in the lives of believers
- *Instill hope* in the hearts of struggling people everywhere

Because He's coming again!

HOWARD
BOOKS

Published by Howard Books, a division of Simon & Schuster, Inc.
1230 Avenue of the Americas, New York, NY 10020
www.howardpublishing.com

Hugs for Women © 1998 by Howard Books
Hugs for Girlfriends © 2002 by Philis Boultinghouse

ISBN-13: 978-1-4165-4187-5
ISBN-10: 1-4165-4187-X

10 9 8 7 6 5 4 3 2 1

HOWARD and colophon are registered trademarks of Simon & Schuster, Inc.

Manufactured in the United States of America

For information regarding special discounts for bulk purchases, please contact Simon & Schuster Special Sales at 1-800-456-6798 or business@simonandschuster.com.

Paraphrased Scriptures by LeAnn Weiss, owner of Encouragement Company
3006 Brandywine Dr., Orlando, FL 32806; 407-898-4410

Hugs for Women
Written and compiled by Mary Hollingsworth, Shady Oaks Studio,
1507 Shirley Way, Bedford, TX 76022
Interior design by LinDee Loveland
Edited by Janet Reed

Hugs for Girlfriends
Edited by Jennifer Stair
Interior design by LinDee Loveland and Stephanie Denney

Thanks to those who shared their stories and friendship with me: Cindy Murray, Sheila Dawson, Maxine Heath, Stephanie Denney, Jana Robertson, Susan Wilson, and Linda Myers.

Scripture quotations taken from the *Holy Bible, New International Version*, Copyright © 1973, 1978, 1984 International Bible Society. Used by permission of Zondervan Bible Publishers.

Stories, sayings, and Scriptures to Encourage and Inspire

hugs®

for
Women

Mary
Hollingsworth

Personalized Scriptures by
LeAnn Weiss

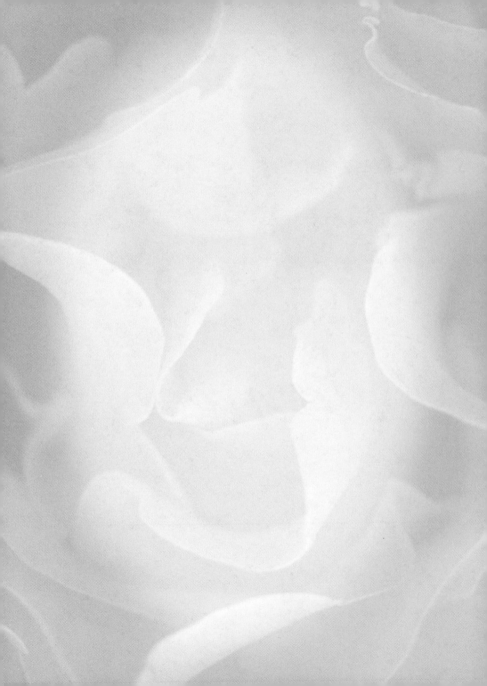

Contents

1

you are woman 1

2

you are amazing 19

3

you are creative 35

4

you are needed 51

5

you are capable........67

6

you are blessed 85

7

you are loved 105

you are

woman

I have made you rich in every way so that you can be generous on every occasion. Your generosity results in thanksgiving to God.

Love,
Your God of Riches in Glory

2 Corinthians 9:11

Do you ever get tired of being a woman? Do you sometimes wish you could just be somebody else for a few days?

When you see mountains of laundry, a list of errands as long as your arm, and a stack of paperwork that needed attention yesterday, would you just like to scream and run out the door? "Here, honey, you be the woman this week. Bye!"

And then you would escape to the freedom of no responsibilities—lunch with a friend at that new bistro down the street and a few hours surfing the net just for fun at www.calm. Peace. Quiet. A leisurely stroll along the riverbank, an hour-long bubble bath with a good book and no interruptions, shopping, and a huge helping of death-by-chocolate dessert (without thinking about the calories). No phones. No beepers. No problems to solve. No PMS. No stress. Ahhhhh . . .

Still, think about it. After a few days with no responsibilities, wouldn't you miss the chubby little arms that wrap tightly around your neck? Wouldn't you miss the secret smile that your husband has just for you? Wouldn't you miss your boss's open admiration for the excellent work you do? Wouldn't you miss being "the one in charge" of the community's Fourth of July event? Wouldn't you miss just being you—an amazing, creative, needed, capable, blessed, and loved woman?

God created you as a woman on purpose. It was no accident, no mistake. He specifically made you to fill a role in this life. He endowed you with carefully chosen gifts and abilities to enable you to fill that important role successfully. He depends on you to be who you were created to be.

I recently discovered that the Old Testament Hebrew word for "Holy Spirit" is a feminine word. And I thought, *Of course! The Comforter. The Guide. The One who teaches and leads. God created woman after the feminine side of His image. We are the gentle spirit of joy and peace that blesses those around us.*

Celebrate! You are God's extended feminine presence in this world. Without you, the world would have an incomplete picture of God. You are woman . . . God's woman.

5

They talk about a woman's sphere

As though it had a limit;

There's not a task to mankind given,

There's not a blessing or a woe,

There's not a whispered "yes" or "no,"

There's not a life, there's not a birth

That has feather's weight of worth

Without a woman in it.

Speaker's Sourcebook

She wandered into their lives,

touched them gently,

and then selflessly wandered away,

never to be seen by them again.

She had amazed them with her

kindness and generosity.

And yet, she was no bigger-than-life heroine.

She was just an ordinary woman—a woman who

gave up her own dream

for someone else's.

the dream

She pulled into town one cool, autumn
afternoon, driving slowly down the main
street. She stopped at the only traffic light
before parking in front of the grocery
store. Carolyn bought bread, bologna,
cheese, pickles, chips, and a Coke. Then
she climbed back into her car and drove to
the edge of town where she noticed a small

park in a grove of elm trees. She stopped there to eat her picnic lunch.

As she dumped her trash into the metal barrel, Carolyn caught her breath. There it was! At long last, after her five-year search, she had found it. Tucked into a secluded spot in the woods stood a little cottage – the one she had always imagined as her writing retreat. A dirt path led from the park to the cottage's front gate.

10

Walking slowly along the path, Carolyn tried to soak up every detail around the small, deserted building. Fallen elm leaves crunched beneath her feet as she walked reverently through the white picket gate and up the old brick walk to the front porch. She tried the front door, and it opened without resistance. A quick inspection made her heart beat a little faster with anticipation. It was the perfect place for a well-known author to find the anonymity and solitude necessary for writing.

Returning to the front porch, Carolyn sat down in the swing and began to push it gently back and forth, back and forth. Its metal chain squeaked softly in rhythm with her thoughts: *It needs new paint, and the shingles on the roof have to be replaced. The roses need to be pruned, and the lawn has to be mowed. But mostly, it needs someone to live in it, love it, care for it. It's perfect! I wonder why it's empty. Is it for sale?*

A sudden impulse sent Carolyn running back to her car. She drove quickly back into town and found the local real estate office. When she asked about the

11

little cottage, she learned that it had been repossessed by the bank; its former owners couldn't pay the back taxes. All she had to do was pay the taxes, and it was hers . . . which is exactly what Carolyn did.

Handing her the key and deed to her new writing retreat, the real estate agent told her about a local fix-it man named Henry. He could help her make the needed repairs. Carolyn stopped to talk to him on her way back to the cottage and arranged for him to begin work the next day.

By mid-December all the repairs had been made. The roof no longer leaked, the cottage had a fresh coat of pale yellow paint and forest green shutters, the lawn had a manicured look, and Carolyn had added

some homey touches inside. It was the perfect haven for writing. Soon she could sit down at her desk overlooking the goldfish pond and begin working on her next novel.

One chilly afternoon as Carolyn swept the leaves off the front porch, she heard a small voice say, "Hello." Looking up, she saw a little red-haired girl swinging on the front gate.

"Well, hello," said Carolyn with a smile. "What's your name?"

"Jenny. What's yours?"

"Carolyn."

"How do you like the house?" the little visitor asked.

"I *love* it. It's just what I've always wanted."

13

"We liked it too," said Jenny. "It looks nice with the new paint."

Carolyn stopped sweeping. "Thanks. Did you live here?"

"Yes, until my daddy died. Then we had to move."

"Where do you live now?" Carolyn asked with concern.

"In the shelter downtown."

Carolyn put down her broom and walked out to the gate. "I'm sorry your daddy died. What happened?"

14

"He was sick for a long time, and he couldn't work. The doctors couldn't make him well. They said he had something called leuke-mia. He died last year, just before Christmas. Then the bank told Mama that we'd have to move. She cried a lot after that."

"I'm so sorry, Jenny. Say, I've got some lemonade inside. Would you like some?"

"Thanks, but I have to go now. My mom will be worried about me. I have to take care of my baby brother while she cooks dinner at the shelter. Maybe I'll come back sometime."

"Please do," Carolyn said quietly as Jenny walked away, glancing back at the little cottage wistfully two or three times before she was out of sight.

Suddenly Carolyn's happy little cottage —her dream—seemed sad and lonely. In her mind she could see Jenny and her family playing in the yard. She could imagine the smell of homemade bread baking in the small kitchen. She could hear the sounds of laughter that now seemed to echo eerily in the trees. And she knew what she had to do.

On Christmas Eve Henry, dressed up in a Santa Claus suit, rang the bell at the downtown shelter. He entered with a happy, "Ho Ho Ho!" and started giving presents to all the children. He handed Jenny a special doll with red hair just like hers, and he had a big, blue rubber ball for Jenny's baby brother.

16

The last thing in Santa's sack was an ordinary white envelope. He walked quietly over to Jenny's mother and said, "Sarah, this is for you." Looking quizzically at him, Sarah took the envelope and tore open the sealed flap. When she removed a piece of paper from the envelope, a key fell into her lap. She recognized it immediately. When she looked at the paper, she realized it was the deed to the cottage—with *her* name on it—marked "Paid in Full."

Tears welled up in her eyes as she pulled out the second piece of paper. The light blue note read, "Please come home. I miss you. Merry Christmas." It was signed, "The Cottage by the Park."

She wandered into their lives, touched them gently, and then selflessly wandered away, never to be seen by them again. She had amazed them with her kindness and generosity. And yet, she was no bigger-than-life heroine. She was just an ordinary woman—a woman who gave up her own dream for someone else's. She was a woman probably very much like you.

17

Reflections . . .

18

_____

_____

_____

_____

_____

_____

_____

_____

_____

_____

_____

you are

amazing

My daughter, you are my workmanship, created in Christ Jesus

M

y daughter, you are My workmanship, created in Christ Jesus to do good works. I've already prepared you in advance for everything I've planned especially for you to do.

Love,
Your God of Purpose

Ephesians 2:10

A woman is not just a person, she's a miracle! Like a cosmic shape-shifter of *Star Trek,* she can transform into anything she needs to be in an instant.

She turns into a nurse at the sight of a scrape or a scratch; in larger emergencies, she's instantly a paramedic.

When trouble comes or the enemy attacks, she becomes the fortress behind which the whole family—even Dad—huddles for protection.

Or she snaps her fingers and changes into a Little League coach, a Girl Scout leader, a homeroom mother, a corporate executive, a financier, a Sunday school teacher, a playmate, a seamstress, a play director, or a volunteer for the March of Dimes.

She is, all in the same day,

a cook, a taxi driver, a boardroom presenter, a maid, a politician, and a referee.

She can be a shrewd merchant at a garage sale, an orator at PTA, a delightful storyteller at the daycare center, and a military genius in organizing the neighborhood against crime.

And, at the wave of a wand, she emerges as Cinderella ready for the ball and waltzes out the door on the arm of her Prince Charming.

In addition, she is often the spiritual heart of the home—guiding, encouraging, leading, teaching, praying. She is God's hands and feet, His laughter and joy, His tears and sorrow. She is the heart of God personified.

There's no doubt about it—a woman is not just a person, she's a miracle!

A nation is not conquered until

the hearts of its women are

on the ground.

Then it is done,

no matter how brave its warriors

nor how strong their weapons.

✾

Cheyenne Proverb

Dorothy was an amazing woman,

like so many other women I've known.

Her determination and faith in God

carried her through to her goal.

the goal

1965. We were in the middle of the Vietnam War. I was a junior in high school in a small rural community in central Texas. And life on this side of the water was good . . . for most of us.

In the class ahead of me—the envied graduating class—was a young man named Robby, a big bruiser and captain of the football team. He had classic good looks, too, which didn't make the girls like him any less. And he studied hard, which didn't make the teachers like him any less. All in all, Robby was a fine man—responsible, dependable, and courageous.

Robby was the only son of Dorothy, a widow who was dying of cancer. Every day at lunchtime and immediately after school, Robby went home to take care of his mom. Although frail, Dorothy always wore a bright smile. And she was so proud of Robby.

28

Dorothy dreamed of living long enough to see Robby graduate from high school. "After that," she said, "I can rest easy." The doctors said she would never make it to the end of May; the cancer had spread throughout her body and continued to grow rapidly. But she always answered with confidence, "Oh, yes, I'll make it. I *have* to make it. I want to be there for Robby."

The spring went by slowly for Dorothy. She endured a lot of pain, and the days dragged while Robby was at school. He wanted to stay home with her, but she wouldn't hear of it. She wanted to see him graduate and be ready to face the world on his own. When word of her goal got around the small town, several women began taking turns sitting with Dorothy during the day so Robby could go to school without worrying about her so much. Dorothy's goal became the entire town's goal.

Dorothy enjoyed helping Robby choose his senior ring, and together they addressed and sent out his graduation announcements. She loved all the preparations for the big

29

day. And she made plans to attend herself, in spite of the warnings from her doctors and friends.

Because the town was so small—982 citizens in all—graduation ceremonies rotated between the three largest churches. In 1965 the ceremony would take place in the church where my father was the minister, and he was the scheduled commencement speaker.

When May 28 finally arrived, parents, teachers, students, and other friends from the community filled the church building. The nineteen seniors lined up excitedly in the foyer wearing their black robes and caps with gold and white tassels. At the arranged cue from the assistant principal, they marched in and filled the first three rows of the church. My dad, the superintendent of schools, and the high school principal entered from the front and took their appointed places on the podium. We were ready to begin.

At that moment, the doors at the back were opened, and two ambulance attendants rolled Dorothy in on a stretcher. A hush fell over the gathering. The raised back of the stretcher supported Dorothy in a semi-sitting position, and she wore a beautiful new aqua-colored dress. Her hair had been professionally done, and her makeup was perfect. She looked beautiful. A brilliant smile lit up her face as she spotted Robby among the seniors, sitting next to the center aisle.

The attendants rolled the stretcher down the aisle and positioned Dorothy next to her son, facing the podium so she could see and hear everything. Robby reached out and took her hand as the speeches began.

The rest of the ceremony proceeded normally, except that we could not take our eyes off Dorothy and Robby. It was a bittersweet experience for everyone but Dorothy, who looked ecstatic the entire time.

At the end of the ceremony, in traditional senior fashion, the graduates cheered and threw their caps into the air. Dorothy cheered and clapped too. Her dream had come true. Her Robby had graduated, and she had lived to see it. No one had dry eyes.

Three days later, Dorothy died. She had held out as long as she needed to. She knew she could rest now, and so she did. She was buried in her beautiful new aqua dress.

Unknown to Dorothy, Robby had received his draft notice two weeks earlier and had enlisted in the marines. A week after his mother died, Robby left for boot camp and then Vietnam. In less than a year, Robby died in action and joined his mother.

Dorothy was an amazing woman, like so many other women I've known. Her determination and faith in God carried her through to her goal. I think of her often, and I know that we can all reach our goals with strong determination and great faith. And someday, when we have reached our goals, we can also rest easy with the Lord.

33

Reflections . . .

3

you are

creative

Celebrate your uniqueness! No one else can do what I've created you to do! Use the special gifts and abilities I have given you to serve others and to faithfully administer My amazing grace as only you can.

Love,
Your Lord of Creativity

P.S. When I appoint, I also anoint!

1 Peter 4:10; James 1:17

Most of the women I know would deny that they are creative. What they really mean is they can't sing, paint, act, or write. Therefore, they must not be creative.

Sadly, through the centuries, our primary concept of *creativity* has been confined to the fine arts. What an enormous mistake! It's certainly not a biblical notion, and its negative effect can never be measured.

In truth, every person is creative in one way or another. The Bible is plain: "God created human beings in his image"—the image of the Great Creator —"male and female he created them." Born with His creative genes, we are endowed with His cleverness and ingenuity. We are blessed with His ability to see finished projects in our minds before we even begin them: events, buildings, garments, budgets, families, meals, missions, and yes, paintings, books, compositions, and dramas.

Our task as His children is to find our personal area of giftedness and talent and to use it for Him.

Perhaps your God-given creativity lies in the
area of teaching, parenting, sewing, accounting,
administrating, comforting, building, computing,
organizing, or landscaping. He may have blessed you
as a creative athlete, musician, caregiver, counselor, chef,
or mechanic.

In His almighty wisdom, God made us to need
each other's creativity. We are not self-sufficient but
interdependent. I may need your mechanical skill
with my car, and you may need my ability to write a
résumé. I definitely need my friend Barbara's talent
for balancing checkbooks, she needs Charlotte's
musical leadership, and Charlotte needs Dr.
Russell's veterinary care for her dog, Cricket.
I need your creative gift, and you need mine.
That's the plan of the Great Creator.

Celebrate your creativity! Don't deny
your gift or your identity as the child
of the Creator. Reach out and touch
others with the gift God has chosen
to impart through you. And
reap the joy!

39

We are each inspired treasures,

with creative gifts to share.

The world needs your gifts!

❦

Sark

The song of praise from one of God's

creative women had done more good

than any punishment could

have accomplished that day

in the hearts of those wayward men.

Lives had been touched.

Hearts had been changed.

Perhaps even souls had been saved.

the song

It had been a typical Saturday night for the busy San Francisco Police Department. Officers had rounded up more than thirty red-eyed, disheveled men for being drunk and disorderly in local bars, clubs, and alleys. On Sunday morning the thirty-plus offenders stood before the judge to hear their deserved punishment.

Some of the men were old, hardened alcoholics who had been before the judge

on numerous occasions and who had no intention of changing their ways. They knew it, and he knew it. Others—first-time lawbreakers—stood with their heads hung in shame. They couldn't even look into the face of the judge.

After the motley bunch was assembled before the judge, the uniformed escorts retreated behind the railing. Quiet settled over the room, and His Honor was about to begin when a strange thing happened. A beautiful, clear soprano voice pierced the silence with the opening strains of "The Holy City":

> Last night I lay a'sleeping,
> There came a dream so fair.

44

Last night! For the guilty group in the courtroom, last night had been a disaster . . . a nightmare or a drunken stupor. The contrast of the song and their own experiences couldn't be ignored. It shocked each man to the core of his being. Then the song continued:

> I stood in old Jerusalem,
> Beside the Temple there.

The judge paused, unable to proceed while the song echoed through the hallowed halls of justice. He asked one of the policemen who was singing and learned that a former member of a famous opera company was awaiting trial for forgery.

As the song went on, every man in the courtroom was overcome with emotion . . . even the hardened alcoholics. A few men dropped to their knees. One young man tried desperately to control himself but finally collapsed against the wall, buried his face against his folded arms, and sobbed, "Oh Mother! Mother!"

The young man's sobbing, blended with the stirring melody, cut to the very heart of every man assembled. Eventually, wiping his eyes, one man protested, "Judge, have we got to submit to this? We're here to take our punishment, but this . . ." Then his voice broke, and he began to cry aloud too.

Although it was impossible to continue the business of the court, the judge did not order the singer to stop. Rather, he sat in silence studying the line of men as the song rose to its magnificent climax:

> Jerusalem, Jerusalem!
>> Sing, for the night is o'er!
> Hosanna in the highest!
>> Hosanna for evermore!

When the powerful final words had faded, a hush settled over the solemn courtroom. The wise old judge looked into the faces of the scoundrels before him—broken, weeping men. Not one of the offenders had gone untouched. Their remorse was plain.

After several moments, the judge cleared the emotion from his throat and quietly advised the men before him to think about what they had heard and change their ways.

47

He didn't call individual cases or impose any kind of fine or punishment. No one was sentenced to the workhouse that day. The men were simply dismissed.

The song of praise from one of God's creative women had done more good than any punishment could have accomplished that day in the hearts of those wayward men. Lives had been touched. Hearts had been changed. Perhaps even souls had been saved.

48

Your creative gift from God might also touch the life and heart of someone around you. God's gifts are powerful, transforming tools, especially when we focus them on reaching out to others with His message of love and grace. Our simple task is to find ways to use our creative gifts, whatever those gifts may be, to praise Him.

Reflections . . .

_____

_____

_____

_____

_____

_____

_____

_____

_____

_____

_____

_____

_____

Reflections . . .

50

_____

_____

_____

_____

_____

_____

_____

_____

_____

_____

_____

_____

_____

4

you are

needed

You are
special a
needed
of the b
of Chris

Y ou are a special and needed part of the body of Christ. Even if you feel weak or insignificant, you are indispensable! I've shaped you with special gifts of service needed for the common good. I've arranged you and gifted you to be needed.

Love,
Your God and Creator

1 Corinthians 12

Those who love you need you in so many different ways, in every area of their lives in which you play a role.

How are you needed?

Your parents need you as a daughter, as a support, as a source of joy. Your siblings need you as a sister, a correspondent, and a partner in family matters.

Your best friend needs you as a listener, as a fun-mate, as a burden sharer, as an encourager and helper.

If you are married, your husband needs you as a loving wife. He may also need you as a tennis partner, bill payer, confidante, and secret keeper. Your children need you as a mother, as a teacher, as a guide, and as a counselor.

Your church family needs you as a spiritual light, a fellow traveler along the Way, a prayer partner, a spring of hope and faith. And all the other people with whom you have relationships need you in the distinctive roles you fill in their lives.

God needs you too. He endowed you with special abilities to serve in

His church and His world. Perhaps He gave you
the gift of hearing the soulful cries of His hurting
children. Maybe He gave you eyes of compassion
that see the desperation in the faces of abused women
and children and the sensitive heart that calls you to
help them. He may have blessed you with a can-do spirit
that inspires others to get involved in projects that look
impossible. Or perhaps He infused you with overflowing
joy that splashes onto anyone who comes near and urges
them onward and upward.

Whatever gifts and abilities He gave you, He needs
you to be at work in His world and His kingdom. No
one else can do what He designed you for in the same
way you can.

55

So many people need you in so many ways,
and no one can take your place. No one else
can play your role. No one else knows your
lines. You are uniquely created to fit in the
special you-shaped space God formed in
His world. Never wonder if you are
needed. The fact that you are here
proves it!

Look for a reason

to need people,

and they will need you

in return.

❧

M. Norvel Young

Divine hugs often have human arms—

a best friend's, a mate's, a parent's.

And because they are

God's personified presence,

it's okay to cry in their embrace. . . .

We need Him.

No one else will do.

no one else will do

Susan was deaf. Suddenly deaf. She had grown up as a hearing person, but at age twenty-one, she awoke one morning to silence. She had only 10 percent residual hearing left in one ear.

I met Susan at church about two years later. An upbeat, outgoing, happy woman, Susan loved people and loved the Lord. She taught sign language for the hearing impaired at the university across the street from our church building.

A few weeks after coming to the church, Susan announced that she would teach sign language classes at the church for anyone who wanted to learn to speak to the deaf. I enrolled primarily because my mom's sister is deaf, and I had always wanted to be able to speak to her more effectively.

Susan and I spent many long hours together practicing sign language—her teaching, me learning. It was a delightful time of sharing.

60

Susan told me that when she first became deaf, she was terrified because she could no longer hear Kelli, her three-year-old daughter. She couldn't hear her cry or scream for help. She couldn't hear her say, "I love you, Mommy." She couldn't hear her laugh or sing. She had to completely retrain Kelli in how to get her attention. Instead of *crying out* for her mother, Kelli had to learn to actually *come* to Susan and show her that she was hurt or needed something. It was a difficult and scary time for both of them.

One Sunday morning as I visited with a friend in the parking lot of the church, I saw Kelli fall down and skin her knee. She had obviously hurt herself, and her little knee was bleeding. But she didn't cry, even though her face showed the pain she felt. Instead, Kelli jumped up and frantically began looking for her mother. She ran past us and into the church, still not crying. I

61

followed her inside to see if I could help. Kelli ran through the foyer looking up into the faces of the women, still not crying.

Stooping down, I stopped her and asked, "Kelli, can I help?"

"No! I need my mama!" she said as she dashed away.

Finally she saw Susan talking to one of the students in our sign language class. Kelli ran to her mother, pulled her face down so that Susan was looking directly into her face, and *then* she began to scream and cry just like any other hurt child. But she had waited until she was actually looking into her mother's face because she knew her mom could not *hear* her cry. It was an amazing and heart-warming thing to watch.

Susan gathered Kelli into her arms and hugged her close, comforting and soothing her as any loving mother would a hurting child. Soon Kelli stopped crying and ran back outside to play with the other children, waving to her mother as she went.

Through the twenty years since then, I have often marveled at what I saw. And I've thought of how we should be like Kelli. She needed her mother. No one else would do. She wouldn't settle for anyone but her. Like Kelli, when we hurt or grieve, we can run straight into the arms of our Father, who will gather us into His divine embrace to comfort and soothe us until the hurt goes away.

Divine hugs often have human arms—a best friend's, a mate's, a parent's. And

because they are God's personified presence, it's okay to cry in their embrace. Through them God will comfort us, dry our tears, and send us back into the game of life . . . bruised, perhaps, but loved and not alone. We need Him. No one else will do.

Reflections . . .

_____

_____

_____

_____

_____

_____

_____

_____

_____

_____

_____

65

Reflections . . .

5

you are

capable

67

You can do it! It's not always easy, but remember, you're not alone. You have an unlimited power source supporting you. You can do all things because I strengthen you!

Love,

The Lord Your Helper

Philippians 4:13

If you are like me, all you have to do is take a long look in the mirror, and your self-esteem drops. After all, I'm fully aware of my faults. I know all the mistakes I've made. My weaknesses and failures are ever before me.

It's no wonder that most people today struggle to keep a healthy self-image. "Self" seems so pathetic and flawed. Why should I, or anyone else, have any esteem for my *self?*

Lack of self-esteem spills over into every area of our lives. Because our images of ourselves are skewed, we *feel* incapable and useless. And because we are so strongly influenced by our feelings, we often *become* incapable. Then we walk around with a hangdog look that says to everyone else, "I'm incapable. I'm useless. I'm worth nothing. Go ahead, step on me."

In truth, this whole scenario is the result of a false image. It all began with a wrong descriptive term: *self-esteem.* I'm sure that word comes from the *Devil's Unabridged Dictionary*—he's the one who wants us to feel incapable and useless. It certainly didn't come from the Word of God.

For several years I've been searching for the right term

to replace *self-esteem* in our vocabulary. I want a word that says, "I can do all things through Christ who gives me the strength." I want a word that says, "God knows that we are made of dust," but "our bodies are the temples of the living God." I want a word that shows that even though we are flawed and weak as human beings, we are strong and capable because the Holy Spirit lives and works through us. I believe that term is *soul-esteem.*

Our *selves* may be imperfect, incapable, and weak, but our *souls* are perfect, capable, and strong through brotherhood with Christ. Our souls are the image of the living God.

When I look in the mirror, I still see *self,* but I also look beyond self to my *soul.* I can finally look the real me in the eye and smile. I'm reminded of 1 Corinthians 13:12: "Now we see but a poor reflection as in a mirror; then we shall see face to face."

So, the next time you look at yourself in the mirror, look past the poor reflection and into the eyes of your soul. And hear Jesus whisper in your ear, "How's your *soul-esteem?*"

71

It seems too adventurous perhaps,
but God is able.
I have no one save the Holy Ghost
to rely upon.
My weak health and lack of ability
seem to deny me success,
but when I am weak, God is strong.
Depending upon him alone,
I go forward . . . though my eyes
are wet with tears,
I must go forward. O Lord,
fill me with the Holy Ghost.
Give me power to move the people.
Amen.

꒰ꕤ꒱

Kiye Sato Yamamuro

When the storm was over,

she was still there,

hanging on to her faith

and determination.

I'm still here

The day before registration at college, Janice—a pretty red-haired freshman—arrived in town by bus. Carrying her single, worn suitcase, held closed with an old belt because the clasps had broken, she walked the four miles from the Greyhound station to the campus on the east side of town.

Janice wandered around campus for a few minutes, just looking at the buildings with amazement. She couldn't believe she was really there. In spite of all the struggles in her life, she had finally made it.

Smiling to herself, Janice went to the administration building and climbed the giant staircase to the front doors. She pulled the huge oak doors open and slowly walked down the hall, taking in the sights and smells. Finally finding the right door, she straightened her skirt, brushed back her hair, and walked into the office. Pearl, long-time administrative aide to the president of the college, looked up and smiled.

"I'd like to see the president, please," said Janice with confidence.

"Won't you have a seat?" asked Pearl. "I'll just see if he's off the phone."

Soon Janice was shown into the president's office. Nervous but determined, she set her suitcase down and blurted out, "Sir, I'm here to go to school. I have my clothes and eighteen dollars. That's all. I can't go back home because I don't have enough money to get there. But I can work; I can work *hard*. And I'm capable of learning anything I need to learn. I want to go to school here more than anything else in the world. Can you help me?"

The president smiled. He was a warmhearted, robust man who loved college kids . . . especially determined ones. "Yes, I think I can," he grinned. And help her he

77

did, by arranging financial aid, on-campus jobs, and scholarships.

That night, Janice called her mother. "Mama, I'm here. And I get to stay! I'm going to school!"

Then for four hard years, Janice cleaned food trays in the cafeteria, mopped floors in the student center, carried huge stacks of books to be refiled in the library, hauled trash out of the administration building, and did numerous other less-than-glamorous jobs. When Janice wasn't working, she was in class or studying.

Unlike most of us on campus, Janice didn't get to join in most of the social activities on campus. She had no free time. She didn't go to parties; she didn't date; she didn't join a social club; she didn't go to the movies on Friday nights. She just worked and studied, studied and worked. And she smiled a lot.

"Hey, Janice, how's it going?" we'd ask.

"Great! With God's help, I'm still here!" she'd say and laugh as she scraped the food off yet another cafeteria tray.

During our senior year, the Hong Kong flu descended on campus with a vengeance. At one point, more than half of the four thousand kids in school had the flu. Between her regular jobs, Janice went from room to room in her dorm, helping the nurse take care of sick girls, cleaning up after them, bringing them medicine and liquids. For two solid weeks she hardly slept.

Then, just as almost everyone was getting well, the flu hit Janice hard. In spite of

Janice's protests that she had to go to work, the nurse put her to bed. "But I can't *afford* to miss work," she moaned. "I need every dollar I earn to stay in school."

When the girls in Janice's dorm heard she was sick, they quickly went into action to repay her kindness. One friend reported to the cafeteria to scrape trays; one went to the administration building and hauled out the trash; another mopped the floors in the student center; and still another pulled her shift refiling books in the library. And they took turns doing it every day while Janice got well. When Janice returned to work, her time cards showed that she had worked four hours overtime during the week she was sick!

Janice and I graduated the same day. When I walked across the stage, I quietly received my diploma. When Janice walked onto the stage a few minutes later, the entire student body rose to its feet and cheered (something that just wasn't done at solemn graduation ceremonies in those days). She had earned our great respect and admiration.

Amazed at the uncharacteristic cheering, the president stopped the formal procession and invited Janice to respond to her classmates at the microphone. Surprised, but happy, Janice walked to the podium, held up her diploma, and said six words: "With God's help, I'm still here!" It was a long time before the president could get the tears

81

and cheers under control so the graduation could continue.

I've thought of Janice often through the years. In spite of difficulties and barriers, she accomplished her goal. She believed in her God, in herself, and in her capability to succeed. And, with God's help, she overcame the mountain of obstacles in her way. When the storm was over, she was still there, hanging on to her faith and determination.

82

Like Janice, we are capable of amazing things with the help of our God and our determination. We are as weak as our fear and as strong as our faith. We simply have to keep up the good fight and say with confidence, "With God's help, I'm still here!"

Reflections . . .

83

Reflections . . .

84

6

you are

blessed

Through my divine power, I have given you everything you need for life and godliness. Don't limit me to your previous experiences; I want to do new things in your life. My plans are far beyond your wildest dreams!

Love,
Your Faithful God

James 1:17; Ephesians 3:20;
2 Peter 1:3

God is faithful to bless us with what we need when we need it. That doesn't mean He always blesses us with what we *want* when we want it. Unlike ours, God's timing is perfect, and the gifts He gives are chosen with divine wisdom and care.

We prefer to believe that blessings always come with "Yes" stamped on them. We struggle to understand how a blessing can be spelled "No." And yet, denial is sometimes the greatest blessing God can give us. His fatherly denial can prevent us from making disastrous mistakes in our lives, like a mother slapping away the hand of a toddler reaching for a hot pan.

How often do we prayerfully hound God to bless us at the time of our choosing? We tap our mental foot and think, *Well, go ahead, Lord; I'm waiting. I need that blessing right now. Could You please let that check come in the mail today?* We become frustrated when it doesn't come when we think it should, and we lapse into doubt and worry. Then we're surprised when God's blessing arrives at the precise moment it's actually needed.

Divine blessings come in small and large packages, expected and unexpected. They come through family, friends, employers, and even strangers. They come in times of joy and times of sadness. Sometimes we recognize them, and sometimes we don't.

Best of all, God can use you to bless someone else. He sends you to a sick friend with words of strength and love. He calls you to bless a stranger with a friendly smile and a helping hand. He inspires you to sing words of blessing, write words of blessing, or speak words of blessing as they are needed by the dying, the lonely, or the depressed.

A blessing is a tiny explosion of joy detonated by God. It ripples through the heart and showers the mind with divine light and hope. Haven't you felt it from time to time? You are blessed by your Father, your *Abba,* who loves you with the overflowing love of heaven. It's a legacy of joy you can pass on to others.

89

Remember the wonderful blessings
that come to you each day
from the hands of a generous
and gracious God,
and forget the irritations that
would detract from your
happiness.

William Arthur Ward

Blessings are strange and

wonderful things.

They are unpredictable.

They can come from both

expected and unexpected places,

as long as we look for them

with open hearts.

the letter

Beautiful and blond, Diane had almost always gotten what she wanted in life. She even got Barry, the man of her dreams. They were happily married and were doing well together. Life was good except for one thing: They had no children.

For the first six years of their marriage, they had tried everything. Finally, the doctor told them quietly that Diane would never be able to have children. Barry took the news with courage, but Diane was shattered. Their perfect happily-ever-after story was seriously flawed.

During their seventh year together, Barry was called up by his army reserve unit and sent to Germany to fight with the Allied Forces. He was stationed in Germany for almost two years. Fortunately, he saw little action and returned home safely. For about three years, things returned to normal—until the letter arrived.

94

The official-looking blue envelope was from the German Immigration Department and addressed to Corporal Barry J. Sanders. Diane turned it over and wondered what was in it, but respecting Barry's privacy, she placed it unopened on his desk with the other mail.

After dinner that evening, Barry went to his office to do some work while Diane enjoyed a long, hot soak in the tub. When she came back downstairs, she found Barry standing awkwardly at the bottom of the steps with the blue envelope in his hand. From the look on his face, Diane knew something was wrong.

"What is it, honey? What's wrong?" she asked.

95

"Diane, there's just no easy way for me to tell you this. So I think you'd better read the letter for yourself." He handed it to her as he sank down in a nearby chair, put his head in his hands, and started to cry.

Dear Corporal Sanders:

We regret to inform you that Gretta Schmidt passed away on February 12 of this year from complications with pneumonia. Before her death, she contacted our office and requested that we make official arrangements for her three-year-old daughter, Ginny Schmidt, to come and live with you as her natural father. Please contact this office immediately with instructions.

Diane stared at the letter in disbelief. Then she looked at Barry's tear-stained face and slowly sat down on the bottom step.

"Is this true? Is this child yours?"

"Yes, I guess so."

"You have a three-year-old daughter, and you never told me?"

"I never knew it until now. It happened during the war. I'm so sorry."

Diane's world crumbled around her. Her perfect husband had been unfaithful to her. More than that, he had a child—something she could never give him—by another woman. She felt as if he had slapped her viciously across the face. She was angry. She was frightened. She was distraught.

Dropping the letter on the floor, Diane ran up the stairs crying and slammed their bedroom door. It was the most devastating sound Barry had ever heard. And he started to cry again.

Barry didn't go to their room that night. Instead, he spent the night in the recliner in

97

the den trying to decide how to put his life back together. He could hear Diane crying until the early hours of the morning. He cried, too, for his war-time stupidity, for Diane, for Gretta, and for little Ginny, who was all alone and probably scared. What was he going to do?

As dawn streamed into the den, he got up and slowly climbed the stairs. Knocking softly on the bedroom door, he opened it and went in. Diane was awake, but her eyes were swollen and red. His heart wrenched when she couldn't even look at him. Finally, he sighed heavily and sat at the foot of the bed.

98

"Honey, I know I've hurt you deeply, and I will regret it for the rest of my life because I love you with all my heart. I won't even try to dignify my actions with Gretta with an explanation. It was inexcusable and wrong. But, all that aside, I have to face the fact that I have a little girl who needs me. She's all alone. Gretta had no family. So, today I'm going to wire the German Immigration Department the money for Ginny's airline ticket to come and live with us. I just don't have any choice. I can only hope that you'll somehow be able to forgive me and help me care for Ginny. I'm sorry . . . so, so sorry."

Without reply, Diane turned her face into her pillow and began to sob. Barry got up from the bed and, with resignation, went down to his office to call the airlines and Western Union.

The next few days were a nightmare. Feeling totally betrayed, Diane couldn't even talk to Barry. He was bringing a strange child—another woman's child—into their house to live. Every time she looked at that child she would be reminded of his infidelity. She just didn't know if she could cope with it.

While she stalked around the house, depressed, silent, and angry, Barry quietly fixed up the second bedroom for Ginny. He coaxed Diane to help him, but she just glared at him and walked out. She would not act happy about this horrible situation.

On Saturday, Diane grudgingly agreed to go with Barry to the airport to meet Ginny's plane. When it arrived, Diane

100

stood back in the waiting crowd. Barry glanced back at her and smiled a few times, but she just stood, arms folded, with a tight-lipped blank stare on her face.

After all the other passengers had deplaned from the Boeing 747, one of the airline attendants walked out with a blond bundle of energy in her arms. She was laughing as the little girl tickled her under the chin. Seeing Barry, the attendant said, "Are you Mr. Sanders?"

"Yes," he answered.

"Well, this is Ginny," she said with a smile. "Ginny, this is your daddy."

Ginny instantly held out her arms for Barry to take her. "Hi, Daddy. I've waited a long time to see you," she said smiling and putting her arms around his neck.

When Barry turned toward Diane, big tears ran down his face. He carried the blue-eyed, dimple-faced Ginny to Diane and said, "Ginny, this is Diane."

Ginny held out her arms to Diane and said, "Oh, you're so pretty! Your hair's the same color as mine. Will you be my new mother?"

Suddenly all of Diane's emotional barriers collapsed. Nothing that had happened was this child's fault. Diane gathered Ginny into her arms and held her close. "Yes, Ginny, I'll be your new mother. And I'll love you with all my heart."

"Me too!" laughed Ginny, wiping the tears off Diane's face.

Barry, Diane, and Ginny stood for a long time just crying and holding each other.

102

the letter

The blessing Diane had always wanted had finally come to her. And even though it came out of sorrow, as days went by, it became the greatest blessing of joy she had ever known. She was a mother to Barry's child after all.

Blessings are strange and wonderful things. They are unpredictable. They can come from both expected and unexpected places, as long as we look for them with open hearts.

Reflections . . .

you are

loved

Your are loved! Sometimes in the midst of trials, you will feel unloved, unappreciated, alone, and abandoned. Even then, know that I am still working and will fulfill My special purpose for you. I'm right there to preserve your life and help you. My love for you lasts forever! Nothing and no one in this universe could ever stop Me from loving you.

Love,
Your Father of
Unfailing Love

Psalm 138:7–8; Romans 8:35–39;
Psalm 36:7

You are loved. Even if you don't always *feel* loved, you are loved. Even if you can't always *see* love, you are loved. Even when you feel alone or lonely, you are loved.

Our society dictates that we show love in specific, tangible, predictable ways—flowers, candy, love letters, rings. These are the acceptable ways of showing love. And yet, the most exciting expressions of love come in those out-of-the-ordinary, surprising, funny moments.

The problem is not that we are unloved; the problem is that we have a limited view of love's expression. We need to broaden our view. We need to improve our lovesight so we don't overlook the subtle, creative, unique ways that love comes to us.

Love behaves in many different ways. One person declares love through hard work, providing for a loved one. Another expresses love by carefully choosing a perfect gift and presenting it at just the right moment. Someone else lavishes tender and meaningful words on a beloved —perhaps in a specially chosen greeting card, a personally composed note, or an unexpected phone call. A fourth shows love through encouragement.

Love comes to you from many different sources too. Can you doubt the love in a tiny boy's handful of pansies plucked from the grumpy neighbor's flower garden? Can you deny the love in a Crayola portrait of Granddad? What mother would miss the love shown by a teenager who cleaned up his room without being prodded? And what about a friend who offers to help you with a crash project at work?

Love may show up wrapped in the funny papers and twine or exquisitely presented in glossy paper and glistening bows. It shines in silent glances from across the room. It might even come in a soft purr or the wag of a tail. It doesn't matter what form it takes, as long as it comes from the heart.

109

Even when all these ordinary kinds of love seem to fail, you are still loved extraordinarily. For God's love letter speaks gloriously to you: God loves you so much that He sent His precious only Son to lead you home to live with Him forever. Oh, yes, you are definitely loved. Never doubt it.

To love and be loved
is like being warmed by the sun
from both sides.

❧

Together Forever

She had lost her mother,

but she had found her Father once again.

And she knew she would be

loved and protected,

no matter what the future held.

the touch of love

The windshield wipers slapped away the pouring rain that blurred Lana's vision as she drove. But they couldn't wipe away the tears pouring down her cheeks. She swiped at them with one hand as she slowed her sports car in the increasing downpour. All the while, she relived the ache of the past few months.

During the frigid days of January, Lana lost the man she most loved—her dad. Someone called her away from her third-grade students to tell her that he was in the hospital, failing quickly from liver cancer. She raced home, packed a few things for a possible extended stay, and drove this same route from Texas to Oklahoma through blowing snow. She arrived just in time to say good-bye before he slipped away.

114

The hole left in her heart by her father's death matched the one left there only a few months earlier by her husband. He had deserted her and filed for divorce. Devastated by his caustic parting words and his flagrant affair with a neighbor, she still felt the pain and humiliation he had caused her.

In the ensuing months, Lana had become lonely and increasingly withdrawn. Her married friends left her out of their social activities, and she found the idea of getting involved with a singles' group unnerving and intimidating. So she spent most of her evenings and weekends grading papers for school or watching television at home, alone.

Then she had been dealt another blow. Her aunt had called this morning to say that her mother had suffered a heart attack and would probably not survive. Once again she found herself flying through bad weather, possibly to say good-bye to mother. "No! No!" she moaned. If her mother died, she would be completely alone. There would be no one left to love her unconditionally, no one she could count on. And the thought made her go cold inside.

Lana brushed at her tears again, then turned up the speed of the wipers. The rain was falling so heavily and fast now that she could hardly make out the white stripes in the center of the road. As she topped a small rise, the wind hit with such force that it scooted her car slightly sideways on the highway, threatening to push into the bar ditch on the side of the road. Lightning split the darkened sky, and thunder seemed to rumble through her car. Lana cried out in fear.

116

She thought about pulling off the road until the storm subsided, but her overwhelming need to be with her dying mother forced her on. She just couldn't stop now.

The storm fit her mood anyway. And if she died in the storm, so what? She was going to be all alone and unloved. Who would care?

"Oh, God!" she whispered out loud, "Where are You? Are You there, or have *You* left me too? Please God, protect me. Keep me safe. Do you still love me, God?"

Suddenly, Lana felt a kind hand touch her left shoulder, and a gentle warmth spread through her. Her inner chill vanished, and a peace she hadn't known in years washed over her heart. Even though she knew she was alone, the hand felt so real and reassuring that she turned her head to look beside her.

117

Of course, no one was there, but what she saw surprised her. Her own reflection

in the rain-splashed window stared back at her. And the most amazing thing struck her: she was smiling . . . really smiling.

That's when Lana knew. She _wasn't_ alone, and she would _never be_ alone. She was loved and would always be loved. Someone did care about her. As long as she remained in God's presence, she knew His divine love would warm and sustain her.

The next day, Lana's mom quietly joined her husband as Lana held her hand. And yet, Lana felt completely at peace. She had lost her mother, but she had found her Father once again. And she knew she would be loved and protected, no matter what the future held.

You, too, are loved by the Father who will never leave you or forsake you. You are His precious child; you will be loved and protected as long as you remain in His presence.

119

Reflections . . .

120

Reflections . . .

121

to

my forever friend,

Sheila Dawson,

who passed from this life

to the next on September 15, 2001,

but who lives in my

heart forever

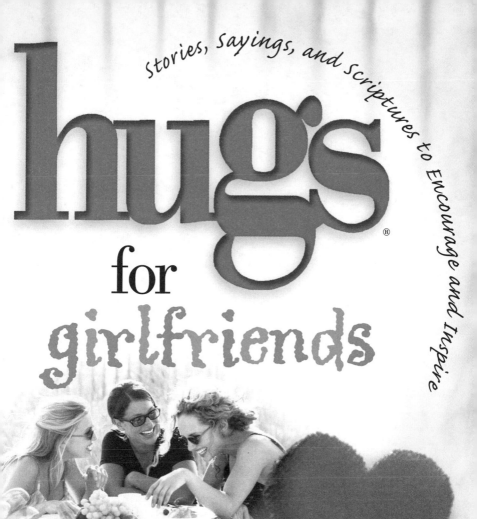

hugs

Stories, sayings, and scriptures to Encourage and Inspire

for
girlfriends

PHILIS BOULTINGHOUSE

Personalized Scriptures by
LEANN WEISS

Contents

chapter 1 • **thoughtfulness** ..... page 127

chapter 2 • **spirit** .... page 147

chapter 3 • **determination** ...... page 165

chapter 4 • **support** .... page 183

chapter 5 • **courage** .... page 199

chapter 6 • **togetherness** ...... page 215

chapter 7 • **trust** .... page 231

thoughtfulness · thoughtfulness

thoughtfulness

chapter 1

Today and everyday, I send you special deliveries of My love and faithfulness. My compassions for you never fail; they are new and waiting for you each and every morning. Come find love and refuge in the shadow of My wings. Feast on My abundance, and drink from My river of delights. In Me you will discover the fountain of life. Blessings will be yours as you spur each other on to love and good deeds.

My priceless & unfailing love,

Your God of Eternal Encouragement

—from Lamentations 3:22–23; Psalm 36:7–9; Hebrews 10:24

Have you ever had a friend surprise you with kindness? It's one of the nicest kinds of surprises in life. Maybe a friend took care of you when you were sick or sat with you during a dark hour and helped you cry. Perhaps she forgave you a serious wrong or loved you when you were being difficult. Whatever the kindness, it required thought and intent. Kindness toward a friend is always more than merely thinking about her; it's doing something to help her.

You've heard the saying: "A friend in need is a friend in..." Now, is it "a friend *in deed*" or "a friend *indeed*"? Either way, it means responding to another's needs with more than words, with more than just saying, "Let me know if I can

inspirational message

do anything." It's *doing* something. Something concrete. Something that requires thought and effort.

Maybe you've seen the bumper sticker that encourages "random acts of kindness." The idea is that one act of kindness can inspire another act of kindness, that act of kindness can inspire another, and so forth and so on. The rippling effect of kindness shared can make a difference that affects the whole world—or at least the world you live in.

And you know, the kindness of friendly deeds doesn't have to be reserved for our closest friends. We can do something really big and really kind for someone we barely know. That's what a friend in deed would do—indeed she would!

The greatest sweetener of human life is friendship.

@

Joseph Addison

Cindy felt an eagerness

and sense of anticipation

that she hadn't felt in months.

Seven months, to be exact.

Love—Out Loud
and On Purpose

● ● ● ● ● ● ● ●

Cindy slammed down the receiver and burst into tears. How could people be so rude when ordering flowers for a holiday that celebrated love?

Cindy knew that it wasn't really the pushy person on the other end of the phone that brought the tears to her eyes. They had been hovering near the overflow rim all day. The unreasonable man had just pushed her last button, and her tears had spilled over.

If Charlie had been there, he would have said something funny and encouraging that would have buoyed her spirits in an instant. But Charlie wasn't there. He would never be there again.

thoughtfulness

Chapter 1

Managing a florist shop during Valentine's season without a Valentine of her own was the pits. This was her first Valentine's Day without Charlie. She hated these "firsts." People said that once she'd made it through a whole year of firsts, she'd be on her way to healing. Cindy didn't believe them. It had been seven months, and she was still having trouble just getting out of bed in the morning. If getting out of bed at seven months took so much effort, how could anyone say she'd be "on her way to healing" at twelve? What did they know?

She had already passed through her first Thanksgiving. Her first Christmas. Her first New Year. All without Charlie. In the upcoming July she'd pass through her first anniversary without him. It would have been their sixth.

She and Charlie had been friends for thirteen years—best friends—counting their years of marriage. They'd met at a Christian student center at Northeast Louisiana University. But at the time, Charlie wasn't a churchgoer; in fact, he wasn't shy about voicing his amazement that anyone would *want* to get up on Sunday morning and go to church. On the morning they met, he and a friend had sauntered into the center right before the 10:30 devotional was to begin. But when they discovered that something "religious" was about to take place, they'd made a very obvious exit.

Cindy's "righteous indignation" had flared, and she followed the boys outside and chewed them out for being so rude. That was the beginning of an inseparable friendship. Charlie soon discovered for himself why Cindy and her friends chose to go to church, and his faith in God grew exponentially.

The last seven months without him had been the most difficult of her life. She'd had difficulties before. That's how life is. But Charlie's death had made her a widow at the age of thirty-two. He'd died suddenly, in his sleep. The doctor said it was sleep apnea. He wasn't even at home when he died. He was "roughing it" at a youth camp where he served as one of the directors. He was doing what he loved to do best: serving others. And all summer he had been serving God in his favorite way—as he used to put it—"out loud and on purpose."

The *physical* pain of grief had surprised Cindy. She'd expected to hurt emotionally, but this pain affected more than her emotions. Besides missing him so much that her whole body ached, she missed being someone's "special

Chapter 1

only." She had been Charlie's special only, and he had been hers. But now she was alone.

Oh, she put on a good face. She was known and loved for her quick sense of humor and her unshakable inner strength. She had one of those deliciously contagious laughs and always had a circle of people around her at church or any gathering—even since Charlie's death. People still counted on her for a good laugh, and she didn't disappoint them.

But there was nothing funny about losing Charlie, and though she didn't allow others to know it, his death had crushed her signature strength right out of her.

Her long day at the flower shop finally came to a close, and she dragged herself to the parking lot and into her car for the ten-minute drive home. At least that was a good thing. She didn't live far from work.

After pulling into her driveway, Cindy trudged to her front door. She thought about what waited for her on the other side: *Just more bills I can't pay and junk mail wanting me to buy things I can't afford.* Her quaint, older house had a mail slot in the front door, and Cindy thought how sad it was to be greeted at the end of every day by a few miscellaneous pieces of impersonal mail. But when she gathered up the envelopes scattered on the floor, she was surprised to discover at least a dozen personal letters. *Personal* letters. Not the kind with see-through windows revealing "creative" misspellings of her name—or even worse: the nameless "Occupant." These letters were not the kind that screamed ridiculous promises in big type. No, these were the kind that had "Cindy Murray" written in a real person's handwriting. The kind that came in odd-sized envelopes with real, licked-on stamps. Personal letters.

Cindy felt an eagerness and sense of anticipation that she hadn't felt in months. Seven months, to be exact. She hurried into the house, plopped down on the couch, and ripped open the first envelope. It was pink. Inside was a beautiful Valentine's card. Before reading the card's message, Cindy opened the card to discover the sender. It was signed, "Someone's thinking of you. Have a happy Valentine's Day!" No name. Cindy checked the outside of the envelope for a return address. Nothing. The postmark revealed that the card came from Monroe—the town where she lived. Cindy turned the envelope over looking for more clues. Nothing. She read the message through several times, trying to find some indication of who had sent the card. Not a thing.

thoughtfulness

Chapter 1

OK, she thought, *let's try another one*. Same thing. A beautiful card expressing generic, but oh so sweet, anonymous love. The next envelope contained a homemade card. This one was even sweeter: "There's all kinds of Valentine-love. Here's wishing you joy and happiness and peace on this day of love." It was signed, "You're not alone."

Card after card shared wishes for peace, comfort, joy... and love. Cindy was dumbfounded. Who would do such a thing? She could tell by the handwriting that they were all from different people. Who would be so thoughtful as to organize this wonderful "card campaign"?

For the first time in a long time, Cindy felt the stirrings of hope in her heart. Maybe she would get through this ordeal after all. Maybe life could be sweet again. Maybe.

As she went about her evening routine of fixing dinner, doing some much-needed paperwork, and straightening up her small, two-bedroom house—the house she and Charlie had shared—Cindy mused over who could have done such a thing. It finally hit her. It was Tara, of course—her best friend. *This is the kind of thing Tara would cook up. I'll call her tomorrow and thank her.*

With a comforted heart, Cindy climbed into bed. Maybe she could sleep tonight without a sleeping pill. If she did, it would be the first time since Charlie died. She slept like a baby—a loved baby.

The next day Cindy went to work with renewed strength. She felt ready to handle whatever the day brought. But when she called Tara to thank her for all the cards, Tara only laughed. "I *wish* I had thought of it. What a great thing for someone to do. I would love to be able to say, 'You're welcome,' but it wasn't me, girlfriend. I wonder who would have schemed up such a thing?" Together they named off all the women in their close circle of friends. Cindy called each of them but received convincing denials from every last one.

That evening when she opened her door, there were *twice* as many envelopes as the day before. *This can't be,* thought Cindy. *I just don't get this.*

It went on like that all week. Each day, there were more Valentine's cards. Many of them were anonymous, but some of them were from children's Sunday school classes at her church. These were signed in childish squiggles. Some contained suckers; others held little candy hearts with corny sayings on them. But they were all filled with love. Other cards came from adult acquaintances at church—but not people who would normally think of her. Someone had prodded them. Someone was behind all this outpouring of love. Cindy's heart was so full, she felt she might burst with joy. Joy she would never have imagined just a few short days ago.

Toward the end of the week, she was getting more than a hundred cards a day. She actually had to push *hard* to open her front door. Unbelievable. *She was loved.*

The Valentine week that had started out so badly was really the turning point in Cindy's healing. Though the cards didn't speak of the special-only love she had shared with Charlie, they spoke loudly and purposefully of *love*— love for her.

But the identity of the Valentine coordinator remained an unsolved mystery until one Sunday, weeks after Valentine's Day, when a college student at church accidentally spilled the secret.

"Mine was the card with the pink hearts on the front and the scripture written inside. Did you get it?"

Cindy snapped her head toward the voice. "What do you mean?"

"You know. The Valentine cards. Mrs. Watley gave us extra credit in speech class for sending Valentine cards to you the week before Valentine's Day. She wrote your name and address on the chalkboard and said she'd add five points to our final grade if we'd send you a card. After she told us about your husband's death and what a special person you are, I would have done it without the extra credit. It was fun to think of someone else for a change. Do you remember getting the cards?"

Cindy remembered all right. Elizabeth Watley. So that's who was behind the outpouring of love.

"Uh…yes, of course I got your card. I loved it! Thank you. Thank you for your thoughtfulness."

But Cindy was distracted. Her eyes were surveying the auditorium full of people, looking for Elizabeth. *Who would have guessed?* Cindy thought. Elizabeth wasn't even in her close circle of friends. Finally, her eyes found their mark. She walked between church pews and past circles of chatting people to get to her new girlfriend.

"Elizabeth."

Elizabeth turned toward the sound of her name. She and Cindy had not made eye contact since before her "card campaign." Now Cindy's eyes locked onto hers, and Elizabeth knew she was found out. No one would ever think that the youthful, perky blonde was old enough to teach a college course, but she was. Elizabeth greeted Cindy with a wide grin and sparkling eyes.

Cindy reached out and put her arms around her new-found friend. Their embrace was long and strong—the embrace of old friends—close friends. Pulling back from the hug, she laughed, "Extra credit? Now, really, Elizabeth, that's too much!"

"My students loved it! I think even they were surprised at how much joy they received from doing a good deed for someone else."

"And the Sunday school classes? And the people from church? How did you manage it all?"

"It was easy! This church is full of people who love you. All they needed was a little prompting. They were eager to reach out to you. It was really no big deal."

"Elizabeth, it was a huge deal! You will never, never know what those cards meant to me." Taking a more serious tone, she asked the question she'd wanted to ask since the first day of her card deluge: "Why? Why did you think of me? You hardly know me!"

"Hey, we girls have to stick together. I've known pain—a different kind of pain from yours—but I know how much a human touch can mean when we hurt. I wanted to touch you in a way that would let you know that you are loved. And you are, you know."

"Yes, I am," replied Cindy. "Girlfriend, why don't you come over to my house one night this week, and I'll show you all the letters your prodding produced. And Elizabeth," Cindy said, her voice catching in her throat, "thank you for loving me Charlie-style: out loud and on purpose!"

spirit · spirit · spirit · spirit · spirit · spirit · spirit

chapter 2

I'll never leave or abandon you. You can count on My goodness and My mercy every day of your life. I love you and will always keep My life-giving promises to you. When you are faithful under trial, you'll receive a crown of life from Me. Anticipate the day when you'll dwell with Me forever!

Eternally,
Your God
& Friend

—from Hebrews 13:5; James 1:12; Psalm 23:6

It's true that what we're made of comes out of us when we're "squeezed." For instance, when you squeeze a lemon, you get sour juice; but when you squeeze a tree-ripened orange, you get sweet nectar. It's the same with us. In our most trying and difficult times, the spirit of who we are at our very center rises to the surface, and what we believe is put to the test.

It's during those testing times that the love of a faithful friend can help ensure that when we're squeezed, something sweet comes out. For a true friend does more than stand beside us during our difficult circumstances; she actually brings out the best in us. She inspires us to dig deep into our hearts and to emerge with a faith

in an eternal God who works all things—even
the pain of this life—together for good for those
who love him. She reminds us that God will supply all the strength we need to get through any trial.
And she does it all without preaching or acting as if
she has all the answers. Instead, she does it by gently
and consistently reminding us of *who* and *Whose* we
really are.

When friends survive the fierceness of a storm
together, their friendship is transformed to one
worthy of eternity. They become united in spirit
and joined together with selfless love for one
another. And when their relationship is
"squeezed," a spirit of never-dying love
and always-there-for-you friendship
comes out.

Women always need other
women to come alongside and
speak their language: the language
of heart and of feelings.

Brenda Hunter

It was as if she were being pressed—and surely she was—and what was coming out of her was Jesus.

Friends Forever

● ● ● ● ● ● ● ●

The atmosphere in the room was almost one of reverence. Family members and friends had gathered around the hospital bed at the request of its occupant. The woman lying limply on the bed radiated strength of spirit and unmistakable peace—in spite of the cancer that was eating away at her life and in spite of the drugging effects of the pain-killing morphine. The doctors hadn't expected her to live through the previous night, but there she was; and though physically listless, she had commandeered the dozen or so people in the room to stand in a semicircle around her bed so that she could see each face and look into each set of eyes.

Chapter 2

Joyce had arrived at the hospital just moments before the gathering. As soon as she'd heard of Sheila's worsened condition, she had jumped in the car and driven the six and a half hours from her Louisiana home to be with her friend of twenty-five years. Her heart ached—physically ached—at the thought of losing her dear friend. She was glad she had made it in time for what was obviously a very special event—an event she and those standing respectfully with her would never forget. As she looked into the eyes of her precious friend, her mind drifted back to the day they had met—so many years ago....

It had been at a women's church gathering. Joyce was sitting in a folding chair, awkwardly balancing a Styrofoam cup of pink punch and a paper plate of finger foods. Although there were several other women in the circle of chairs, they were all quite a bit older than she; and after a quick hello and "We're so glad you're here," they had gone to sit with their own circles of friends, unintentionally leaving Joyce alone and lonely.

That's when the smiling young woman had plopped down beside her.

"Hi, I'm Sheila," she said. "So you're the new preacher's wife."

The two women were obviously of the same generation. Both had long hair, parted in the middle, with no bangs—the generic hair style that was so popular in the early seventies. The only difference in their hair was that Sheila's was blonde and Joyce's a dark brown.

Joyce was usually referred to as "the *little* preacher's wife" and was glad to be identified without the discriminating "little." They called her husband "the little preacher" not because of his slight frame, but because of his age. He'd come to the 150-member church straight out of seminary. He was a mere twenty-five years old, and Joyce was twenty-four. Though the older women in the congregation doted on their new little preacher and his wife, Joyce longed for a friend—a *girlfriend*—with whom she could share her life.

Joyce returned Sheila's smile. "That's me—the new preacher's wife. I'm glad to finally meet someone near my own age."

"I know what you mean," Sheila replied. "My husband and I just moved here, and I don't know a soul."

Chapter 2

It hadn't taken long for the two young women to discover how much they had in common. Both shared a strong faith in God, both had come from large families, and both had married men who'd moved them far from their childhood homes. But it was their shared pregnancies that had sealed the friendship. They shared morning sickness, shopping for maternity clothes, and the thrill of feeling the first flutter of the miracles growing inside them.

Now, the child Sheila had been carrying stood at the foot of his mother's bed, a member of the privileged circle.

Sheila smiled weakly as she took in the sight around her. One at a time, she locked eyes with each individual, whispering his or her name between labored breaths. Each spoken name resonated with a lifetime of love. Then summoning strength from what could only be a divine source, she spoke to the entire group: "Thank you for coming and sharing the Lord with me today. May God bless you all."

The dying one blessed the living. The weak spoke courage to the strong. "Sing 'It Is Well with My Soul,'" she rasped—each word requiring precious energy. The emotion-filled voices around the bed struggled to put air and melody behind the words formed by their mouths.

When peace like a river attendeth my way,
When sorrows like sea billows roll;
Whatever my lot, Thou hast taught me to say,
"It is well, it is well with my soul."

Sheila sang along with them, mouthing each word with deliberate intent. The faith that had always marked her demeanor and way of life radiated from her even now. In fact, her faith infused the weary hearts around her and bolstered their battered souls. More than once during the song, Joyce's voice caught in her throat at the thought of losing this dear friend.

When they began singing the third verse, Sheila raised her hands in worship, and her voice filled with more power and strength than humanly possible—given her circumstances. But her circumstances were overpowered by her faith.

And Lord, haste the day when my faith shall be sight,
The clouds be rolled back as a scroll;
The trump shall resound, and the Lord shall descend,
Even so, it is well with my soul.

Sheila was the only one in the room not crying. She was beaming. How her unquenched spirit could beam through her incapacitated body was beyond explanation. It was as if the very Spirit of God were oozing out of her. It was as if she were being pressed—and surely she was—and what was coming out of her was Jesus.

With an incomprehensible clarity of mind and strength of spirit, she requested song after song that expressed her unwavering faith and devotion to God. Not a hint of self-pity, not an ounce of regret could be seen on her face—and it was evident to all that her face truly reflected the content of her heart.

After thirty minutes or so of praise and worship, Sheila fell into a contented sleep. The holy atmosphere lingered, and her loved ones embraced one another and spoke of the wonder they had just experienced. Visitors said parting words to family members, and soon, everyone was gone except Sheila's husband, Malcom; her son, Sean; her daughter and son-in-law, Jeanelle and Aaron—and Joyce.

Joyce turned her attention to Sheila's teary-eyed husband. She had to ask: "What are the doctors saying?"

"Not much," Malcom replied. "They're not giving us any hope that she'll live, but no one seems to know how much time we have left with her."

Malcom's eyes were filled with a pain for which there is no medication. He hadn't slept for the last seventy-two hours. "Every time she wakes up, I can see in her eyes that she's looking for me. I don't want not to be here when she opens her eyes." He looked out the window into the night as he continued, "But it's almost more than I can stand to watch her like this." He paused and looked straight into Joyce's eyes. "I'm so glad you're here. Seeing the light in her eyes when she saw you in the circle did my heart good."

"She's an amazing woman," Joyce said with awe. "Her body looks so frail, but her spirit just seems to *blaze* out of her." Malcom's eyes flooded with new tears—part of the endless supply of grief.

"Listen, Malcom," Joyce said, "you have got to have a break. Why don't you and Sean go rest in the lobby? Jeanelle and Aaron can catch a little sleep on the bed in the corner, and I'll sit by Sheila. If she wakes up and looks for you, I'll send Aaron to get you. I promise I won't leave her."

Reluctantly, Malcom agreed. Sean put his arm around his father's shoulder, and the two men walked out the door. Aaron and Jeanelle settled onto the narrow bed, and Joyce pulled a heavy, vinyl-covered chair as close to Sheila's bed as possible. She couldn't take her eyes off her dear friend. This was the first chance she'd had to be alone with her.

Joyce had seen Sheila just ten weeks earlier. At the time, Sheila's hair had just begun to thin from her chemotherapy treatments, but she'd had it cut in a cute style that made the most of the hair she had left. Sheila had been a bit tired, but not too tired to take a walk. Walking was something they'd always loved to do together. But it was really the talking part of walking that they liked. They'd easily shared their hearts that day—just as they always did when they were together. Both had every reason to be confident that Sheila would weather her treatments and finish strong.

But now Sheila's appearance was a stark contrast to the hope of recovery she'd portrayed that day. Her delicate head was almost entirely bald. Only a few stray wisps of reddish hair remained. The most startling aspect of her appearance were the purple sores that covered her face, her head, her neck, her chest, her arms—her whole body. Once again, Joyce thought of life without this friend, and fretful tears sprang to her eyes.

Joyce watched her friend's chest rise and fall. Sometimes the span between breaths was so long that Joyce feared Sheila's chest would not rise again. But she soon grew accustomed to Sheila's sporadic breathing and the wheezing sound in her throat.

For the next three or four hours, Joyce dozed off and on. At about two in the morning, she was jolted awake by the sound of Sheila coughing. The coughs racked her tiny body. Joyce rushed to her side and lifted her torso off the mattress and at an angle that seemed more comfortable. When the coughs finally subsided, Joyce put a cup of water with a straw to Sheila's lips. "You want a drink, sweetie?"

In response, Sheila pursed her lips around the straw.

"Come on, Sheila, suck. You can do it....There you go." Joyce eased her friend back onto the special air mattress that supported her body.

"Is that you, Joyce?" Sheila asked weakly.

"Yes, girlfriend, it's me," Joyce said as she moved her face closer to Sheila's.

"I'm so glad you came to see me. I can't believe you came…"

Chapter 2

Joyce was overcome with love for her friend and at the same time felt suffocated at the thought of losing her. *Lord, I don't want to lose this friend!* her heart silently cried; but to Sheila she said, "Of course I came. I love you." Joyce tenderly kissed Sheila's gaunt cheek and stroked her slick head, smoothing her thin sprawl of hair. "Sheila, you're so beautiful. I was thinking about you and praying for you the whole time I was driving up to see you. You're one special woman, you know."

"I love you too," Sheila whispered as her heavy eyelids fell back into place. "Thank you for sharing the Lord with me today."

With a full heart and an unexpected peace, Joyce sank back into the uncomfortable chair, smiling contentedly. It was obvious she would never lose this friend. Theirs was a friendship that would last an eternity.

determination • determination

determination

chapter 3

My eyes are on you. I've chosen you, calling you My friend. I've blessed you with My love, calling you My own. I'm close to you when you're brokenhearted; I save you when your spirit is crushed; I choose to bear your burdens daily. Come out of the darkness into My confidence. Walk in My sacrificial love.

Blessings & love,
Your Heavenly Father

—from Psalm 34:15; 1 John 3:1; Psalms 34:18; 68:19; 1 Peter 2:9; Ephesians 5:1–2

A friend is *determined* to help. Absolutely determined. She knows that there are times when all the stops must be pulled out, when logic must be defied and common sense thrown to the wind. And a friend knows how to recognize those times.

A determined friend will act on a wild impulse to do you good. She will operate on a supersense that knows when it's time to push ahead in spite of the obstacles. A determined friend will risk failure; she'll defy danger; she'll take a chance.

At its purest form, true friendship means self-sacrifice; it means putting the interests of a friend above our own. Jesus went so far as to say that the ultimate expression of love is laying down our lives for our friends—just as he laid down his life for us, his friends (John 15:13).

Most of us are stronger than we think we are, more capable of sacrificial giving than we know. God has created us with a huge capacity for giving, with a heart for selfless loving. When He gives us the opportunity to put it all on the line for a friend, He will provide us with the determination we need if we will just step out in faith.

There comes a time when—if friendship is to move to the next level—a risk must be taken, an impulse must be acted upon, or a hare-brained idea must be carried to completion. There comes a time when the only thing we have propelling us forward is sheer determination.

The determination of a dedicated friend.

Empathy and acceptance are
two of the most effective ways of
carrying out Christ's command to
love each other as He loves.

Kathy Narramore

For a moment Maxine's resolve wavered, but when she looked into Carmen's hopeful eyes, she knew this was something she had to do.

Mother by Birth, Friend by Choice

● ● ● ● ● ● ● ●

Her whole life was inside that purse.

Carmen was fifteen years old—a very difficult age even when among friends and familiar surroundings—but right now, Carmen had neither.

It was summertime, and her family had just moved to a new town. Not only did Carmen not have any friends, she didn't even have a house to live in—much less her own room.

The Heaths had moved to West Monroe, Louisiana, because her dad had gotten a promotion at work. It may have been an upward move for her dad, but it was the worst thing that had happened to Carmen in her fifteen years.

She didn't know a single person, which meant she didn't have even one person she could call *friend*.

Until they could find a home of their own, her family of four was living with Artie—a big-hearted, single woman from the church they attended. Though Artie's heart was big, her house was small, and there wasn't even room inside her home for their suitcases. Those remained in the car. Carmen felt like a vagrant. Her family was living out of a car.

Her purse was her constant companion. In it was her whole identity. Her learner's permit was in her wallet. This alone was a huge deal. Then there was the promise-key necklace that her father had given her on her fifteenth birthday. He'd taken her out on a "date"—just the two of them—and he'd talked with her about keeping herself pure for her future husband. The key was the key to her heart, which she would one day give to her husband. And finally, there was the love note. Carmen knew it didn't really mean anything in terms of a real relationship, but it meant the world to her heart. It was simple and sweet and spoke of innocent devotion. The things in that purse were the most important things in her world.

Carmen's mother, Maxine, hurt for her eldest daughter. She knew the move had been hard on her and that beginning her sophomore year at a new high school would be even harder. So one Monday morning, just a few days before school started, she suggested that the two of them go shopping. They'd buy Carmen some new clothes for school and have lunch together at the mall. Carmen gladly accepted her mother's invitation, and the two of them headed out the door.

The shopping trip really did the trick. Carmen hadn't felt this good since their move. There's nothing like some new clothes and a fun lunch to lift a young girl's spirit—or an old girl's, for that matter. For the first time since the move, Carmen felt like she might make it after all.

On the way home, Carmen gathered up the few things she wanted to take into the house into one bag. She put her purse in the white plastic bag with her new purchases and tied it up tight.

The meal that evening was especially jovial, and Carmen happily helped her mom and Artie clean up. When she crawled into the bed she shared with her sister, she easily fell into a contented sleep.

When Carmen woke up the next morning, the first thing she wanted to do was try on some of her new outfits. She looked around the bedroom for her white sack but couldn't find it. She finally remembered that she'd left it on an out-of-the-way kitchen shelf. She went straight to the spot. It wasn't there. *Maybe someone moved it last night when we were cleaning up.* "Mom," Carmen called to her mom in the next room, "where's the sack I brought in from the car last night?"

"I think I saw it on the kitchen shelf."

"Yeah, that's where I left it; but it's not there now."

"Hmm," Maxine said as she walked into the room. "I'll help you find it. Artie may have moved it when we were cleaning up."

After fifteen minutes of searching, Maxine had an unsettling thought: *What if Artie threw the sack in the trash, not realizing what was in it? No big deal; I'll just dig it out.* Not wanting to alarm Carmen unnecessarily, she snuck a look into the kitchen garbage can. It had obviously been emptied either late the night before or early that morning. She casually walked out onto the carport to check the dumpster. It was standing at the curb's edge—its cover flipped open. A horrific awareness began to dawn on Maxine. The bag—and Carmen's purse—had been picked up and taken to the dump. Maxine felt sick to her stomach. Losing the clothes they'd bought the day before was not a significant loss, but losing Carmen's purse was. *Everything important to her is in that purse.*

Lost in her thoughts, Maxine didn't hear Carmen come out the door. Carmen had come to the same conclusion her mother had and had checked all the inside trash cans and was now coming out to check the dumpster. At the sight of the open, empty bin, Carmen ran to the street, screaming, "Mom, they've taken my purse! They've taken it to the dump!" Carmen sunk to the ground and cried. "We've got to get it back, Mom," she pleaded. "We've got to go get it right now!"

Maxine was beside Carmen in seconds, bending over her, trying to put her arms around her to console her. "No, Mom, no!" Carmen frantically screamed as she jumped to her feet. "We've got to go right now!"

"Carmen, I have no idea where the dump is. I don't even know what garbage service Artie uses. We'll get you another purse."

But even as she said the words, Maxine knew that the *purse* wasn't the issue—it was what was inside the purse; it was what its contents represented. To Carmen, that purse held her whole identity.

Carmen was almost hysterical. "Mom, we have to get that purse back! We just have to! It's got my permit and the necklace Daddy gave me—and my letter…" Carmen dissolved into tears. No matter what Maxine said or did, Carmen was not to be comforted.

A resolve began to form in Maxine's mind. *This child needs that purse. I don't know how I'm going to do it, but I am determined to get that purse back.* Something told her that this was one of those times when logic and common sense had to be defied and all the stops pulled out. "Carmen," she said with more confidence than she felt, "we're going to figure this out. If there is any way possible, we're going to find that purse."

Carmen looked at her mom in surprise. "Really? You're really going to get it back for me?"

"I'm sure going to try. Let's see if we can find the name of the garbage company on the dumpster." But a careful search of all sides revealed nothing. "Come on, Carmen; we're going to make some calls."

Maxine ran toward the house with Carmen right behind her. She raced to the drawer that held the telephone directory. She quickly flipped to "Garbage" in the Yellow Pages. A growing sense of urgency began to overtake Maxine. She knew that if she were going to find that purse before it was covered in mounds of garbage, she would have to act fast. It may already be too late.

After calling several garbage companies, asking about pickup schedules in Artie's neighborhood, Maxine finally found the company she thought had emptied Artie's dumpster and carried off Carmen's purse. She frantically explained the situation to the woman on the other end of the line. Maxine expected the operator to think she was crazy, but the woman said that Maxine's urgent request was not all that unusual. The problem was that there was no way to contact the truck driver. Their only hope was to get to the dump before the truck did and try to intercept the driver as he entered the gate.

Carmen and Maxine flew to the car and headed for the dump, following the woman's instructions. Carmen's hysteria had calmed, but her tears fell in a steady stream. "Thanks, Mom. Thanks for doing this. I can hardly believe that we're actually going to the dump. I know this is crazy. Thanks, Mom."

Maxine drove faster than she knew she should, and she kept her mind focused on her scribbled directions to the dump. There was no time for getting lost. Finally, they came to the last turn. "BFI Waste," the sign said, and they turned off the old highway onto a dirt road. Racing up the road as fast as she dared, dust flying behind them, Maxine finally came to a stop at the gate.

Even before they opened the car doors, Maxine and Carmen were overwhelmed by the pungent smell. Neither of them had ever been to a garbage dump, and it was much worse than either could have imagined. But Maxine got out of the car and walked over to the small structure that housed the gatekeeper. Feeling completely foolish, Maxine told her story one more time, and once again she was surprised at how helpful and sympathetic her listener was. The man flipped through a large, worn spiral notebook for several minutes until he found the number of the truck that had collected trash from the address Maxine had given him. Truck number 39. She and Carmen had gotten there before the truck had.

Maxine let out a sigh of relief. All they could do now was wait for the truck and try to talk to the driver as he approached the gate.

After waiting for just a few minutes, truck number 39 came rolling toward the gate. Maxine got out of the car and waved down the driver. She told her story for the third time. The driver didn't hold out much hope that they would find their bag, but he told them they could follow him into the dump yard, watch where he dumped his load, and sift through the trash.

For the first time, it dawned on Maxine that they were actually going to have to get *into* that awful-smelling, squishy, gross mound of garbage. For a moment Maxine's resolve wavered, but when she looked into Carmen's hopeful eyes, she knew this was something she had to do. This was the time to go the extra mile.

She put the car into gear and followed the truck as he made his way to his dumping site. Their eyes were glued to the truck as the bed lifted and the sloppy mess slid out of the truck and onto the heap.

"OK, Carmen, are you ready?" Maxine asked.

"Oh, Mom, it's so gross. I think I'm going to throw up."

"We've come this far. We can't back out now. Come on; we can do this."

Keeping their shoes on to protect their feet from broken glass, they rolled up their pant legs and walked out onto the mountain of refuse. Holding their noses and fighting against the urge to gag, they walked as lightly as they could, not wanting to sink down into unknown horrors below the surface—which was horrible enough in itself. They were walking on rotting food, dirty diapers, and unidentifiable nastiness. The hot sun intensified the sickening aroma. They knew they couldn't stand this for long, so they searched diligently, gingerly lifting little bits of trash at a time.

After about only ten minutes of searching, Carmen spotted the white plastic bag, tied neatly, just as she'd left it. "I found it, Mom! I found it!"

Their repulsion turned to immediate glee. Mother and daughter hugged each other and jumped up and down on top of the trash heap.

"Mom, I can't believe you did this for me! This is the nicest thing anyone has ever done for me. You're more than my mom, you're my friend—my best friend!" And with one final squeeze, she shouted, "I love you, girlfriend!"

support · support · support

chapter 4

I've redeemed you, personally calling you by name. I satisfy your desires with good things and renew you, blessing you with peace. Watch Me restore your soul and lead you in paths of righteousness. I'll encourage you and strengthen your heart in every good deed and word, enabling you to accomplish all things.

Empowering you,
Your God
of Restoration

—from Isaiah 43:1; Psalms 103:5; 29:11; 23:3–4;
2 Thessalonians 2:16–17;
Philippians 4:13

*F*ortitude. It's a good word. It has a bit of an old-fashioned ring to it, but it means something good in every era. Fortitude is about strength and stick-to-it-iveness. It's the quality of a friend who holds on tight and refuses to let you slip away. Fortitude is about hanging around when a friend has failed. It's about supplying support to someone whose strength is gone.

Do you remember the Old Testament story of Moses when the Israelites were fighting the Amalekites? As long as Moses held up his hands, the Israelites would win; but if he let his hands drop, they'd lose. It didn't take long for Moses to get tired, and so two of his friends—his brother, Aaron, and his friend Hur—

held up Moses' hands when he no longer
had the strength.

That's what friends do. They hold up our
hands when the battles of life get too difficult,
and they stay beside us, giving us their unwavering
support and encouragement.

The truth is: we all do some pretty stupid things
in our lives—every single one of us. Maybe we make
bad choices in a relationship; perhaps we break a
confidence by telling something we promised not
to; maybe we tell a little lie—or a big whopper.
Whatever it is, we all do things that need
forgiving, that need the gentle mercy of a
faithful friend. That's when we need a
friend of fortitude. A friend who will
stay beside us and refuse to let us
slip away.

The glory of friendship...is the spiritual inspiration that comes to one when he discovers that someone else believes in him.

Ralph Waldo Emerson

You are a pearl of great price. Your mind, your soul, and your sweet, sweet heart are more precious to us and to your heavenly Father than all the pearls in the world.

The Pearl of Great Price

● ● ● ● ● ● ● ●

The three girlfriends hunched over the glass counter, evaluating their options. When they stood up straight to get the attendant's attention, their varying heights were like stepping stones—short, medium, and tall.

"It's got to be *substantial* looking," said the medium-height woman. Crystal was wearing a yellow silk pantsuit, and her short, wavy, brown hair matched her dark brown, intentional eyes. "It needs to be big enough to communicate *substance.*"

"And, of course, it must be beautiful," said Becky, the tall one. Her height and slender frame communicated the sort of artistic gracefulness that cannot be counterfeited. "We want her to *want* to wear it all the time."

191

Chapter 4

Leah, the shortest of the three, had soft, blonde hair that framed her pleasant, soft face. But behind the softness was an unmistakable strength. Leah carried herself as one who'd endured the storms of life with unusual class. "And we want a chain that's strong *and* beautiful. We don't want our 'pearl of great price' getting lost because of a flimsy chain."

It wasn't their ages or backgrounds or interests that bound these three women together. These women were "work friends." And it was another work friend's need that brought them together this day. Two weeks earlier, their younger colleague had swallowed an entire bottle of sleeping pills in an attempt to take her life. It was Becky's phone call that had saved her.

"Hey, girlfriend, what ya doing?" Becky had chirped into the phone.

"Nothing…much…," Diane had mumbled weakly.

"You don't sound too good, Diane. Are you all right?"

"Sure…I'm just…fine…," Diane had answered haltingly.

Even though Diane was twenty-five and Becky thirty-six, the bond between them had grown substantially during the last four years of working together. And Becky knew Diane well enough to realize that she wasn't all right.

"I'm coming right over, hon," Becky had told her, trying to sound calm and cheerful.

Diane had not been herself the last couple of weeks. Unexplained tears had sprung to her eyes on more than one occasion, and her whole demeanor had exuded a deepening sadness. Becky had taken her to lunch to cheer her up, but it hadn't made much difference.

Now, Becky's concern turned to fear, and as she neared Diane's apartment, the fear was escalating into panic. By the time she pulled into the driveway, her intuition was screaming that something was not right. Diane's front door was unlocked, so Becky charged in, her long legs speeding her to Diane's bedroom. Her first view of Diane lying limply across her bed confirmed her fears. Becky's heart skipped a beat when she saw the empty prescription bottle lying on Diane's nightstand. She glided to Diane's bed and sat down beside her lethargic friend. Grabbing Diane's hand, Becky felt for a pulse. It was barely perceptible, and her breathing was shallow and erratic.

Becky nervously called 911, and in just a few short minutes an ambulance and medical workers were at the door. It didn't take long for them to assess the situation and get

Diane into the ambulance, where they began immediate treatment. Becky followed the ambulance to the hospital and stayed with her friend until she was settled in a hospital room for overnight observation.

The next day, the three friends went together to visit Diane during their lunch hour. They came away determined to get their young friend the counseling she needed and to figure out some way to communicate to her just how special she was.

It was on their way back to work that they came up with the idea for the necklace. They'd been trying to think of Bible verses that communicate God's love when Crystal thought of the story of the pearl of great price. "We can get her a pearl necklace and explain to her that to God—and to us—*she* is a pearl of great price."

It seemed like the perfect idea, and that's why the three of them were deliberating together in Lee's Jewelry. After examining every pearl-drop necklace in the store, they still didn't find one that communicated the strength and beauty and substance they were looking for. So when the jeweler offered to make a custom necklace for their friend, they were thrilled.

"I have the chain you want here, but I'll have to order

the pearl. FedEx can get it to me tomorrow, and I'll have your friend's necklace ready the day after that."

Driving back to the office, the three girls schemed and planned how and when to give Diane her necklace. Becky, the artist among them, offered to design a card. Leah, the production manager, said she'd arrange for a quiet booth in Diane's favorite restaurant. And Crystal, the writer, said she'd write a message explaining the pearl's great value.

Diane's first day back at work was the same day the necklace was due to be ready. Diane wasn't at all suspicious when Leah asked her to join them for lunch. It was sort of a "welcome back" lunch, Leah told her.

The four friends—their ages ranging from twenty-five to fifty—settled into a cozy booth. "Lunch is on us today, Diane," Leah declared. "We are so glad you're back with us and feeling better!"

Diane hung her head. "I'm so ashamed of what I did and all the fuss I caused. It's really kind of embarrassing. But you have treated me—well, normal. And that's what I've needed. Thank you for being there for me."

Leah reached across the table and put her hand over Diane's. "We love you, Diane. You are so special to us."

"OK, enough of this mushy stuff," Becky said. "Let's order some lunch!"

After the waitress took their orders, Crystal reached into her purse and pulled out a blue and yellow gift bag and Becky's "designer" card. She set them on the table and pushed them across to Diane.

"What's this?" Diane asked, searching the eyes of her friends for a hint.

"Read the card," Becky said gently, "and you'll find out."

Diane's eyes were already tearing up as she took the card out of its distinctive envelope. The eyes of her three friends were on her as she read.

Diane—The Pearl of Great Price

In Matthew 13, Jesus used the figure of a beautiful pearl to portray the immense value of the kingdom of God. And like the merchant who gave up all he had to make the beautiful pearl his own, God has given the most precious of all that is His—His own Son—to make you His own.

Diane, you are a pearl of great price. Your mind, your soul, and your sweet, sweet heart are

more precious to us and to your heavenly Father
than all the pearls in the world.

Today, we give you this pearl necklace to con-
vey to you your immeasurable value to God and
to us. As you wear it around your neck, we want
you to be continually reminded of your special place
in God's heart, of the honor that He has bestowed
on you through His Son, and the privilege He has
given you of honoring Him with your body, your
heart, and your life.

Remember this: "You were bought with a great
price; therefore glorify God with your body" (1
Corinthians 6:20).

We love you Diane,
Crystal, Becky, Leah

The tears were flowing unhindered as Diane looked into
the eyes of her older girlfriends.

"Go on," urged Crystal. "Open the box."

Diane pulled apart the blue tissue paper and reached
into the bag. She took out the little, white box and slowly
removed the lid. She let out a gasp. The necklace inside

truly was "substantial." She lifted it off its cushiony resting place and fingered the pearl in wonder.

"Will you put it on me?" Diane asked Leah.

"Sure, turn around….There, it's on."

Diane raised her hand to touch the necklace. "It's perfect," she said. "How can I say thank you?"

"Well…," said Becky, "you can start by going to the appointment we've made for you with a counselor."

"You did what?" Diane asked.

"We've made you an appointment with a counselor, and we expect you to keep it. OK?"

"I don't mean to sound ungrateful…but I can't afford a counselor."

"That's already been taken care of. Your only job is to get better," Crystal insisted. "Now, will you go?"

"How could I not? Of course, I'll go."

Now Diane was crying in earnest. She grabbed Leah's hand and put it on the table, and then she reached across for the hands of Crystal and Becky. Her friends saw more hope in Diane's eyes than they had seen in a long time. Diane squeezed their hands tightly and said with confidence, "I think I'm going to make it, girlfriends. I really do."

courage · courage · courage
courage · courage

chapter 5

Give Me everything that worries you, and watch My perfect love dismantle your fears. Be strong and courageous, realizing that I'm with you through your struggles. Absolutely nothing is too difficult with Me, your Friend. I'll sustain you and will never let you fall.

Love,
Your Ever Present Helper

—from Psalm 55:22; 1 John 4:18;
Joshua 1:9; Jeremiah 32:17; Psalm 46:1

Did you know that courage is contagious? It is. And there's no one better to catch courage from than a familiar friend. Walking into a pitch-black room can be terribly frightening when you're all alone; but if you've got a friend by your side, the darkness somehow loses its power, and your fears melt away. Surviving a relational hurt can seem impossible alone, but the support of a friend puts things in a whole new perspective.

Sometimes you won't even be able to tell who sprouted the courage first, for it flows back and forth between two friends without need to recognize its beginning. When we see courage shining from a friend's heart, it may be hers or it may be our own we see reflected there.

When the apostle Peter walked

on the water at Jesus' bidding, he stood on the courage of another. He saw courage and confidence in the face of his friend and Lord, and that courage became his own. And when Peter's courage failed, the hand of his faithful friend reached out and rescued him from the churning waters.

When your courage falters, find a friend and borrow some of hers. And when someone you love is shaking in her boots, extend your own steady hand to infuse strength and peace into her frightened heart. Courage can be transferred from one heart to another simply by a shared look of understanding or a gentle touch of encouragement. The courage given you by heaven above is not intended for your strengthening alone—it is meant to be shared with a friend.

Sometimes when we can't even express our pain, the language of a girlfriend goes way beyond what can be uttered.

Chonda Pierce

She'd thought that
everything was under
control and that they
were both ready.
Until now.

A Labor of Love

● ● ● ● ● ● ● ●

As she hurried down the long hallway, Tammy could hear Jana screaming. *What have I gotten myself into?* she asked herself. *What made me think I could be Jana's labor coach? She's only in the very beginning stages of labor, and she's already out of control. What do I think I'm doing?*

But Tammy had made a promise, and, of course, she would keep it.

Jana had come to work at the lawyer's office where Tammy was office manager more than a year ago. They had become friends right away. They had little in common except for their love for God, which not everyone at the office shared. Tammy's children were in college, while Jana's were in elementary and preschool. Tammy loved camping and hiking and just about anything that got her dirty. Jana, on the other hand, was an indoors girl and much preferred convenience to nature.

When Jana had discovered that she was pregnant, Tammy was the first person she told after her husband. They had gone out to lunch to celebrate—something they both loved to do. Although she and Wayne hadn't exactly been *trying* to get pregnant, they hadn't been trying not to. This would be Jana's third child, and she and Wayne were delighted!

But when Jana returned from her first doctor's visit, her delight had vanished, and she was worried and upset. She asked Tammy to meet her in the break room. Sitting down at a corner table, Jana began to cry. "I've been so excited about this pregnancy that I hadn't even thought about insurance until my doctor's visit this morning. Wayne and I let our insurance lapse a few months ago so we could catch up on some bills. The cost of having a baby has tripled since I had Kristen! The insurance lady at the doctor's office said we could make monthly payments on the doctor's fee, but there's no way we'll be able to pay for the epidural. That costs *hundreds* of dollars. I had an epidural with my first two, and I'm scared to death at the thought of going through labor without one. I can't believe I let myself get pregnant. This is one of the stupidest things I've ever done."

Tammy had been listening quietly. Now she moved her chair closer to Jana's and took Jana's hand in hers. "Listen, Jana. I have an idea. I'm not sure it's a good one, but it's an idea. When I had my babies, epidurals weren't as common as they are today. And besides, you know me; I like to do things the natural way, so I took Lamaze lessons and had both kids without any medication. I was taught to think of labor as 'hard work' instead of 'pain,' and I learned some techniques that helped me feel like I had some control over the labor process. I can't say it didn't hurt; but I can say that, all and all, it was a really positive experience."

"But I'm not like you, Tammy," Jana wailed. "You love all that natural, do-it-yourself stuff. You're braver than I am—and stronger too. There's no way I could have a baby without any pain medication."

"Who's saying you can't have *any*? You just can't have an epidural. There are plenty of other drugs they can give you to ease the pain."

"I don't want the pain just *eased!* I want it *gone!* And besides, I've never heard of anyone here going to Lamaze classes. I don't even think they're available."

"I never have either—that's where my idea comes in. What if I became your Lamaze coach? I've still got my old books—there might even be some updated versions we can buy. I can teach you the breathing and relaxation techniques, and I can coach you through labor. What do you think?"

"I think you're crazy! And I think there's no way I can do this!"

"Yes, you can, Jana. With the combination of Demerol, Lamaze, and a little coaching, you can do this. I know you can!"

"Well," Jana finally relented, "I really don't have much choice. When do we start?"

"When I took the classes, we didn't start until six weeks before due date. Until then, we'll get you some books, and you and Wayne can start reading up on Dr. Lamaze."

That was seven and a half months ago. Tammy had taught Jana the three breathing techniques and all about effleurage, focal points, and how to relax during contractions. She'd thought that everything was under control and that they were both ready. Until now. Now her confidence was replaced with doubt: *What have I gotten myself into?*

As she walked into Jana's room, Jana let out one more piercing, long scream and grabbed hold of Wayne's arm with a fierce strength. Wayne's eyes pleaded with Tammy to do something to make it better—and to make it better quick.

Tammy let her purse slide off her shoulder and onto the floor and took her place opposite Wayne on the other side of Jana's bed.

"Jana, look at me," Tammy instructed calmly. "Let go of Wayne's arm, look into my eyes, and do what I do."

Jana obeyed instantly. She watched Tammy take in a deep "cleansing breath" as the contraction ended, and Jana did the same. Tammy stroked her arm, just like they'd practiced in their relaxation exercises, and Jana began to relax.

"Wayne, how many centimeters is she dilated?"

"The nurse checked her just a few minutes before you got here and said she was at four."

"OK, Jana, that means we're going to use the second stage of breathing. When the next contraction comes," Tammy said with feigned confidence, "we'll be ready.

Remember what we talked about—you're going to ride it like a wave. We can tell from the monitor when your contraction peaks and begins going down. Wayne will let you know when you're on your way down, so you'll know the end is in sight. All you have to do is ride the wave one contraction at a time. Your job is to relax; your body's job is to get that baby out into the world. Are you ready? There's another one coming."

Jana nodded as she took her preparatory cleansing breath right along with Tammy. "Good girl. Now keep your eyes on me. And remember, start out slow, speeding up as the contraction intensifies. Keep your breathing shallow and even. OK, here we go." Tammy began the breathing they had practiced so many times: "Hee, hee, hee, hee, whoo, hee, hee, hee, hee, whoo…"

"You're on your way down," Wayne finally said. "You'll be through this one in no time."

After a final cleansing breath, Jana said excitedly, "I made it! I made it through the whole thing without screaming. It's really a lot better that way!"

Jana's boosted confidence bolstered Tammy, and the three of them "labored" together like this for the next four hours—each doing their part. Only twice—during the transition stage—did Jana's eyes fill with panic as she felt herself losing her rhythm, but not once did she scream. The contractions finally got so close together that they were right on top of each other, and Jana began to feel the urge to push. Wayne ran to get the nurse.

"You're ready," the nurse said after checking her. "As soon as I can get the doctor in here, you can start pushing."

"I don't remember how to push!" Jana hollered, panic settling in on her face.

"That's OK, Jana. I remember how," Tammy reassured her. "All you have to do is watch me and do what I do."

The doctor rushed into the room as the next huge wave hit Jana, and together she, Wayne, and Tammy got through the first push. With the fourth push, the baby's head emerged, and with the sixth, she was out! A girl! A beautiful, bawling, pink little girl.

"Oh, let me hold her," Jana exclaimed. As the nurse placed the slippery baby on her chest, Jana began to laugh and cry at the same time. "She's gorgeous! She's perfect! I can hardly believe it!"

"Now I know why they call it labor," Jana exclaimed. "I've never worked so hard in my life. If it hadn't been for you, girlfriend, I never would have made it. You were so calm and confident. Your courage rubbed off on me."

"I'll let you in on a little secret," Tammy confessed. "I was scared to death. I got my courage from you! After you got things under control, you rode those waves like a pro."

"Oh, I almost forgot!" Wayne said. "I brought my camera. We've got to get some pictures! Tammy, will you take some of me and Jana and the baby?"

It was hard focusing the camera through her tears, but Tammy managed to get some great shots.

"Now, let me get one of you three girls," Wayne suggested. Tammy snuggled up to Jana and her precious bundle. "OK, on the count of three. One...two...three..."

Simultaneously, Jana and Tammy turned to face one another and then back to the camera: "Girlfriends!" they shouted, and Wayne snapped the picture.

Jana cuddled her baby and smiled at her best friend. "We did it, girlfriend! We did it!"

togetherness · togetherness

chapter 6

Make no mistake—you are dearly loved. I've crowned you with loving kindness and compassion. Imitate Me, making love the motto of all your actions. Experience the joy of treating others as you'd like to be treated yourself. Remember, you're an ambassador of My amazing grace!

Compassionately,
Your God of Love

—from Psalm 103:4; Ephesians 5:1;
1 Corinthians 16:14; Matthew 7:12

There's an old song called "One Is the Loneliest Number." And it's true. Of course, being alone isn't always bad—in fact, sometimes it's very good—but being lonely…well, that's something altogether different. It's not good to be lonely.

And that's where friends come in. A friend makes sure we don't have to do the important stuff alone. She makes sure that we don't cry alone, that we don't celebrate alone, and that we don't fall down alone.

Wise King Solomon had it right when he said, "Two are better than one: If one falls down, [her] friend can pick [her] up" (Ecclesiastes 4:10).

Life is full of "fall-downs." We fall down when we fail a test at school. We fall down when a relationship sours. We fall down when we botch a really important responsibility at work. We fall down when we treat a friend unkindly.

Sometimes it's not easy to stick by the side of a fallen friend. At times it may seem that a friend doesn't deserve our devotion—and she may not. Maybe she's done us wrong or said something unkind about us. But when she's at her worst, she needs the touch of her friend the most. It's the "fall-down" times that prove the authenticity of a friend.

A true friend is there for the fall downs; a genuine friend picks up the fallen one. Then, the next time around, the fallen one will take a turn at picking up the other. Two *are* better than one.

Every friend is like a flower
in life that is admired for its
exquisite beauty and
God-given design.

Ginny Hobson

"We weren't trying to
be disrespectful—
we were just doing
the best we could with
what we had."

Finding a Place

● ● ● ● ● ● ● ●

"Uh...excuse me," Hannah muttered, not lifting her head. It wasn't uncommon for Hannah to bump into other students as she walked through the halls of the old high school: head down, eyes on the floor, shoulders hunched over the stack of books she clutched to her chest. She'd only lived in Molene for three weeks, and she'd already earned the nickname "Hunchback Hannah" for her curved-back posture.

A freshman in a new high school, Hannah felt isolated and alone. She dragged her feet across the floor as she headed toward her most hated class of all—P.E. There she would be forced to put down her protective books and put on an ugly, unflattering one-piece gym suit. The powder blue suit had little cap sleeves, bloomer shorts—the worst!—and snaps up the front. And the slightly too-high, sewn-in waistband achieved two embarrassments at once: It accentuated her hips and de-accentuated what little breasts she had.

Most of the girls weren't outwardly cruel, but she was all too aware of the whispered references to her hated nickname and the stares at her kinky brown hair. It was 1969—before the days of hair products that tamed unruly hair and before the days when naturally curly hair was in style. Even worse than the rude stares, though, were the eyes that looked right through her—as if she weren't even there. The only way she survived her loneliness was to imagine herself back in her old hometown, at her old junior high, with her old friends. Only there could she escape the pain of being alone.

Daydreaming about after-school bike rides with her best friend, Karen, Hannah mindlessly turned the dial on her locker-room combination lock—right 3, left 7, right 4. After taking off her starched white blouse and navy pleated skirt, she reached into her locker to pull out her gym clothes. That's when it hit her. *I forgot my knee socks! I can't believe it! I forgot my white knee socks!* She dug frantically through her locker, hoping against hope that maybe she'd find an extra pair of the socks that were worth two points of her five-point daily "dress-out" grade. Two points for the jumpsuit, one point for her shoes, and two points for her socks. Five points total. Five points meant an A. Three points meant a C. And to Hannah, a C was unacceptable.

Not only would she get two points off her grade, she was mortified at the thought of standing out from the crowd. A disproportionate panic began to press in on Hannah. *What am I going to do! WHAT AM I GOING TO DO?*

"You forget something?"

"Huh?" Hannah asked, trying to rein in her panic and focus on the face the words were coming from.

"Did you forget something?"

"Uh, yeah. I forgot my white socks."

"Oh, I hate it when I do that. Two points down the drain—just over a stupid pair of socks!" The girl actually laughed as she said it.

Hannah didn't think it was a laughing matter.

"My name's Chris, Chris Thompson," she said. "What's yours?"

"I'm Hannah Gibbs." Hannah remembered seeing this red-headed girl with the easy laugh in her biology class.

Chapter 6

Hannah had heard some of the girls making fun of Chris for her bright red hair and her freckled face. She, too, was in the "out" crowd.

"Well, Hannah, I have an idea. You've got the blue knee socks you wore to school. I'll let you wear one of my white socks, and I'll wear one of your blue socks."

"What good will that do?"

"It'll do a whole letter grade of good, that's what. Mrs. Pilcher will have to give you one point for your one sock."

"You're crazy. Whoever heard of wearing one white sock and one blue sock?"

"So we'll be the first ones. We're innovative!"

Hannah didn't have any better ideas, so the two girls dressed quickly and ran outside.

"I feel like a total nerd," Hannah whispered as they slipped into the last of four rows of girls, who were standing like a military troop awaiting inspection.

"That's because you *are* a nerd," Chris retorted. "But haven't you ever heard the ancient, wise saying: 'Two nerds are better than one'?"

Hannah laughed in spite of herself. She was surprised at the strange feeling of camaraderie she felt toward Chris. It was one thing to be a lonely nerd, but it was something else entirely to have a co-nerd standing beside her, sharing her "weirdo" status.

It didn't take long for the girls on their row to notice the odd-looking pair. Their snickers drew the attention of girls in the front rows, and soon they were surrounded by stifled giggles and pointing fingers. Mrs. Pilcher, distracted from her inspection routine by the ruckus around her, searched the rows of girls and quickly found the center of everyone's attention.

"What is going on here?" she barked.

At the sound of her voice, the troop of girls did the best they could to regain their composure. They slapped their arms stiffly to their sides and tried desperately to control themselves, but little eruptions of laughter cropped up in one spot and then another.

Mrs. Pilcher was not deterred by the hilarity around her. She marched intently toward the center of the commotion and stopped in front of Hannah, with her face just inches from the trembling girl's. "Miss, uh…" In vain, Mrs. Pilcher searched the class role on her clipboard for a clue to the girl's name. Of course she didn't know Hannah's name. Hannah was one of the nameless faces. Nothing about the girl warranted attention: She wasn't particularly good at anything, and she'd never caused any trouble. With so many girls to keep up with, some just had to be ignored—or at least that was Mrs. Pilcher's unstated philosophy.

"Well, girl, speak up! What do you mean by purposely disregarding the dress code?"

"I, uh…I mean…," Hannah stammered.

"It was my idea, Mrs. Pilcher," Chris spoke up.

Until that moment, Mrs. Pilcher hadn't even noticed that Chris, too, had violated the dress code. Chris could have easily kept her mouth shut and avoided the reprimand. Hannah was taken aback by the generosity and kindheartedness of this girl who barely knew her.

"You see," she continued, "we only had one pair of white knee socks between us, so we decided to share. We weren't trying to be disrespectful—we were just doing the best we could with what we had."

Mrs. Pilcher's demeanor softened, but she retained her firm tone. "Well, your spirit of cooperation is to be commended. You each have a B for today's dress-out grade. But whoever forgot your socks—don't let it happen again!"

"Yes, ma'am," the girls answered in unison.

Hannah could hardly believe the turn of events. Even though she and Chris had been laughed at and whispered about, she felt an unexpected hope growing in her heart, and for the first time since she'd been at Molene Junior High, she felt as if she might actually find a place for herself here.

After class, the two girls walked together to the locker room, sharing little bits about themselves in the way that newfound friends do. As they changed back into their school clothes, they made plans to meet after school.

"I'll see you later, nerd," Chris teased.

"Yeah, weirdo," Hannah teased back as she picked up her schoolbooks and pulled them to her body. "We did the best we could with what we had—and it worked!"

As they parted ways, Hannah walked with a new deliberateness in her step, with her head held high and her back straight and tall.

trust • trust • trust • trust • trust

chapter 7

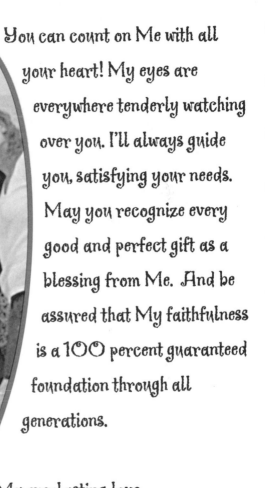

You can count on Me with all your heart! My eyes are everywhere tenderly watching over you. I'll always guide you, satisfying your needs. May you recognize every good and perfect gift as a blessing from Me. And be assured that My faithfulness is a 100 percent guaranteed foundation through all generations.

My everlasting love,
Your Trustworthy God

—Proverbs 3:5; 15:3; Isaiah 58:11;
James 1:17; Psalm 119:90

Webster defines *trust* as "assured reliance on the character, ability, strength, or truth of someone; one in which confidence is placed." That simple definition sums up the essential qualities of a friend.

A friend is someone you can rely on, depend on, *trust* to know the truth of you and love you anyway. A friend is someone you can tell a secret to and know—without a doubt—that she won't tell, even when she gets mad at you. A friend is someone who will allow you to have a bad day and not write you off as a lost cause. A friend is someone who will go the distance with you and help you finish the course, no matter how rough the terrain. A friend is someone who will see past your grouchy words to your hurting heart. A friend is someone you can trust.

But trust is a fragile thing. It is not easily attained—in fact, it can take years of proving— yet it can be lost in a single day. It's then that the real test of friendship emerges. For if after suffering betrayal by a trusted friend, we can look to heaven's example and forgive—and not only forgive, but also trust again—we will have in our hearts the ingredients of a precious friend.

Trust is like gold that is purified by fire. Only after it has come under the testing heat of difficult times, hurt feelings, and even failure does it provide the foundation for a friendship that has the strength to survive a lifetime.

An encouraging friend is a
lifeline to steady a floundering
heart, to bring sunshine to a
cloudy day, and to deliver
a blessing just looking for
a place to land.

Susan Duke

"I have a little baby
boy for William
and Kammy. Do
they still want one?"

Angels Watching over Me

Linda stood in the corner of the bookstore, tears streaming down her face. She'd stopped to get a birthday card for her best friend, Kristen, when her eyes fell on the plaque. Its words broadsided her heart:

> Not flesh of my flesh nor bone of my bone
> But still miraculously my own
> Never forget for a single moment
> You didn't grow under my heart but in it.

Why can't it be that way for William and Kammy? her heart cried. *Why can't they find a baby to adopt?*

Linda's daughter, Kammy, and her son-in-law, William, had been married for fifteen years. For four of those years

they'd tried to have a baby. Hormones, shots, distant doctor visits—nothing had worked.

Then came three failed adoption efforts.

For the past year and a half, Kammy had endured a horrific emotional roller-coaster ride. Dizzying heights of joy were followed by fierce curves of disappointment and harrying plunges into despair.

All of this was on Linda's heart as she held the plaque in her hand. She sadly placed it back on the shelf and walked out of the store empty-handed—not having the heart to sift through the cheerful birthday cards. She'd have to pick one up later.

As she walked through her carport door, the phone was ringing. *Richard is always so good to call when he's out of town*, Linda thought as she reached for the phone.

"Hello," she said, trying to sound collected and calm.

"Hi, Linda, this is Karen."

Linda strained to recognize the voice. *Karen who?* she thought.

"Linda," the woman continued, "I have a baby for William and Kammy."

Linda's mouth dropped open, and the phone slipped

from her hand. She scrambled to pick it back up and then slumped into the nearest chair.

Oh, that Karen. It was the lawyer who had worked with William and Kammy on two of the failed adoptions. "Karen, what are you talking about?"

"I have a little baby boy for William and Kammy. Do they still want one?"

She said it like someone might say, "I have a puppy for you. Would you like to have it?"

"Of course, they still want a baby; but what are you saying?"

Karen explained, "The last time I went through an adoption effort with Kammy, I promised her I wouldn't call her until I had signatures from both parents and the five-day waiting period was over. Well, I have a baby, and three of the days have passed. The father has already signed, and I feel very confident that I'll get the mother's signature the day after tomorrow.

"But there's a problem," she continued. "The baby needs to leave the hospital tomorrow. I wouldn't want you to be seen taking him from the hospital, so I could pick him up after work tomorrow and take him home with me. But I need you to pick him up tomorrow night from my house and keep him at your house until the mother signs. Will you do that?"

Stunned, Linda replied, "Of course, I will. I just can't believe it's true!"

After all the details were worked out, Linda hung up the phone and collapsed on the couch. Her hands began to shake, her heart raced, and she felt dizzy and weak. When the phone rang again, she about jumped out of her skin. It was Richard. Her words came tumbling out, but as the story was told, an overwhelming urgency overtook her. "Richard, you've got to pray for me. You've got to pray that I can do this, that I will be calm, that my blood pressure won't go up, that I can keep the secret from Kammy, that no one at her office or from her church will find out. You've got to pray!"

As she talked of prayer, she could feel her heartbeat slowing down to normal and her shaking hands regaining their composure. When she hung up the phone this time, she dropped to her knees, folded her hands, and bowed her head on the couch. "Lord, You've got to help me. I don't have a clue how I'm going to do this. But I know this is of You—we've prayed for this child for so long—and I know You will give me the strength I need to get through this."

Linda spent most of the night in prayer: prayer for the birth mother and father, prayer for the lawyer, prayer for herself, but mostly prayer for the baby, that what was best would be.

Feeling the need to keep up a front of normalcy, Linda didn't break her weekly lunch date with her friend Kristen. To cancel would arouse Kristen's suspicion. Besides, she had to keep busy or she'd go nuts.

Kristen and Linda had been friends for years. Now, one look at Linda, and Kristen knew that something was going on with her friend. After they were seated and had ordered their ice tea, Kristen looked Linda in the eyes: "OK, girlfriend, what is going on?"

"What do you mean? Everything's fine," Linda lied.

"Listen to me, girl," Kristen said as she reached across the table and took Linda's hand, "I haven't been your friend for all these years for nothing. I know when something's going on with you. What is it?"

It took only a few seconds of thought for Linda to decide that Kristen could be completely trusted with her secret. "Kristen, you're not going to believe this, but if you promise not to tell anyone, I'll tell you. I've got to tell someone!"

Kristen's eyes grew wider and her grip on Linda's hand

tighter as the tale unfolded. "That is just too much! Part of me knows that I shouldn't be so surprised because this is what we've been praying for all these years, but the other part of me is just flattened!"

"Can you believe that I'm actually going to have him in my house tonight? I haven't taken care of a baby in years." A look of sudden realization fell over Linda's face. "Oh, no! I don't have any clothes for him—or bottles or anything!"

"Well, we can solve that problem. We'll do one of the things we do best. We'll go shopping!"

The two friends, giddy with excitement and nervousness, went to Wal-Mart. Linda knew she shouldn't buy too many things—in case the adoption didn't work out—so she just got a couple of simple gowns, some booties, disposable diapers, and a few other basic supplies.

"But we've got to get one special gown to dress him in when you give him to Kammy," Kristen insisted. "Let's go to Alice's Baby Shop and get something soft and wonderful. You can keep the tags on until everything is signed and sealed."

Satisfied with the idea, the friends picked out the softest, bluest, most little-boyish gown they could find. And of course, they had to get little shoes and socks and a blanket to match.

Kristen kept Linda busy all afternoon to help her pass the time. When it was time to pick up the baby, Kristen went home, but only after Linda promised to call her if she needed any help.

Richard wouldn't be home until the next day, so Linda went to Karen's house alone. Her hands trembled as she rang the doorbell. In just a few seconds, she would meet her potential grandson.

The tiny baby slept through the whole exchange, and Linda was relieved when she finally had her little charge under her own roof.

She took the sleeping baby to her bed and laid him in the hollow of an orthopedic pillow. He was so tiny. So helpless. So dependent on her. But in spite of the grave responsibility she felt, a strange calm hovered over Linda's house and over Linda herself. She was normally fretful and worried in stressful situations, and her blood pressure could go dangerously high when she felt tense. But an unearthly tranquility filled her heart and mind. She knew the peace was not her own, but from God. And another thing: She felt a certainty, an assurance, that heaven had sent a band of angels to fill her house and heart with peace. They filled the air like a sweet perfume.

trust Chapter 7

All night long, the baby and Linda slept together on her bed. He woke once to eat, but after slurping down one of the bottles of formula Karen had brought home from the hospital, he dutifully burped and went straight back to sleep.

When the baby woke crying at five the next morning, Linda was instantly awake. Today was the day the mother was supposed to sign. But the thought that would normally have sent her blood pressure flying didn't even send a fretful feeling to her heart. God was in control. Angels had watched over them all night long. Whatever happened today was going to be within God's will.

At seven o'clock, the phone rang. It was Kristen. "How was your night? How is the baby? How are you doing? Can I come over and help you rock him while you wait?"

"Well, let me see if I can get that straight. Fine. Good. Great. Sure, come on over, I'd love the company!" Linda laughed. "Oh, and Kristen, bring your video camera. I'm praying we'll need it."

All morning long, the two friends took turns holding, feeding, burping, changing, and watching him sleep. Karen called as soon as the signing was completed. It had gone off without a hitch. Unbelievable. Well, actually, it was quite believable. God had gotten them through the difficult years and now He was giving them the desires of their hearts.

It was time to call Kammy at work. "Kammy," Linda began, "Dad and I need to talk to you. I want you and William to meet us at your house."

"Sorry, Mom, but I already have plans for lunch," Kammy cheerfully replied.

"Whatever you have planned will have to wait. You have to meet your dad and me at your house."

Now Kammy was worried. "What is it, Mom? What's going on?"

"Just meet us there in half an hour."

But Kammy wasn't the only one Linda had to call. It was time to let the other grandparents in on the secret. "Meet us at William and Kammy's at twelve sharp," Linda instructed with an uncommon confidence.

"Come on, Kristen; it's show time."

At twelve o'clock, five cars convened in William and Kammy's driveway: Kammy's, William's, Karen's, Richard's, and the other grandparents'. Then Linda and Kristen pulled in, making sure theirs was the last car to arrive.

The group had gathered on the front lawn, watching Linda park the car, waiting to see what would happen next.

As the two friends walked up the sidewalk with their precious bundle, they were met with six pairs of wondering eyes. Karen was finally free to speak. "Kammy, I told you that if I ever got you a baby, I'd make sure all was signed and settled before I told you about it. Well, it's all signed and settled. Meet your new son."

As Linda handed her grandson to his mom, Kristen wrapped both arms around her friend and squeezed her tight. "You did it, Grandma! You protected your daughter from potential pain, and you loved your grandson even before you knew he was yours. And now, I've got a present for you that I've been saving for this very day." From behind her back appeared a beautiful gift bag.

Linda reached in and pulled out a plaque—just like the one she'd seen in the bookstore just two short days ago:

Not flesh of my flesh nor bone of my bone
But still miraculously my own
Never forget for a single moment
You didn't grow under my heart but in it.